WHOM SHALL I FEAR

D0913615

To Sandy,
thank you so much
for your support
God Bless

Lavon Morris-Grant
4/01

WHOM SHALL I FEAR
A Spiritual Journey Of A Battered Woman

Lavon Morris-Grant

MCS PUBLISHING, NEWBURGH, NEW YORK

WHOM SHALL I FEAR
A Spiritual Journey Of A Battered Woman

By Lavon Morris-Grant

Published by:

MCS Publishing
PMB 219
56 North Plank Road, Suite 1
Newburgh, NY 12550-2116

Printed in the United States of America

Library of Congress Cataloging-in-Publication Data

Morris-Grant, Lavon, 1962—
Whom Shall I Fear : A spiritual journey of a battered woman / Lavon Morris-Grant
p.   cm.

ISBN 0-9707995-3-5
I. Morris-Grant,/ Lavon, 1962— 2. Abused women— 3. Spirituality

Library of Congress Catalog Card Number 00-193571

Cover design by Lavon Morris-Grant
Photography by Christopher Hubble

*This book is dedicated to
my three beautiful children,
Marques, Corey, and Sheriah
who, along with God, gave me the
strength and courage to go on*

And to

*Reverend J. Edward Lewis for having the
vision long before this book was
a reality*

Contents

Acknowledgments

I thank my Lord and Savior, Jesus Christ for bringing me a mighty long way.

I thank each of my children; Marques, Corey, and Sheriah, whom I love dearly, for their bravery, and patience, and trusting that I would create new realities for them as I struggled through the writing of this book.

I thank my mother, Clarastine (Jordan) Akbar, for life, and passing her strength as a woman to me. I thank my father, William Morris for also giving me the gift of life. I thank my sisters; Tonja Morris, Jeanette Morris, Yvette Morris, Andrea Morris, Fatima Akbar, and Sharon Shipman-Drake, and my brothers; William Morris, and Troy Morris for being a special part of my journey. I also thank all of my Auntie's, Uncle's and cousins for all of their love and support.

I give a special thanks to the Reverend J. Edward Lewis for believing that I could write this book and teaching me to look within myself for wholeness, by loving and valuing who I am, as well as Cynthia McCollie-Lewis for affirming the power of my writing and encouraging me to join a writer's group to enhance my communication skills.

I give my love and thanks to the writers' group that I was a part of for two years, especially Kate Shaughnessy, Kris Garnier, and to Marie Whitman for being there every step of the way; page-by-page, chapter-by-chapter, and all the late night phone calls. A very special heartfelt thanks to Steven Lewis, my teacher, editor, and mentor for his patience, gentle guidance, and his many extraordinary gifts and talents as a writer.

I thank Laura Kelly for being my friend, reading through the entire manuscript many times, and helping me to understand the true meaning of recovery. I also thank Janet Cains for gracing me with her presence and Godly wisdom.

I thank Cynthia Barton for all her encouragement of support, and not abandoning me at a time when I needed her friendship the most, and Nola Hatton for her love of my children, and teaching me how to be a better mother.

I thank Barbara Deutsch for her angelic spirit and for copyediting the book, and Elizabeth Davis for making the connection.

Acknowledgments

My thanks also go out to Christopher Hubble, Katherine Whitman, and Amy Aiken.

I thank the staff at NCAC in Newburgh, particularly Margaret Bodison for offering me affordable day care when all hope seemed lost, and to the staff at the Domestic Violence agency in Orange County, especially Eileen Maddock, Daria Zepko, Miriam Arroyo, Elaine Holmes, Denee Taylor, Ursula Forum, and Maurene Vickner TerBush.

I thank all the women from the Newburgh support group who touched my life with their stories, strength, and courage.

The Lord is my light and my salvation
Whom shall I fear?
The Lord is the strength of my life; of
Whom shall I be afraid?
When evil men advance against me
to devour my flesh,
when my enemies and my foes attack me,
they will stumble and fall.
Though an army besiege me,
my heart shall not fear;
though war break out against me
even then will I be confident.
One thing I ask of the Lord,
this is what I seek:
that I may dwell in the house of the Lord
all the days of my life,
to gaze upon the beauty of the Lord
and to seek him in his temple.
For in the day of trouble
he will keep me safe in his dwelling;
he will hide me in the shelter of his
tabernacle
and set me high upon a rock.
Then my head will be exalted above
the enemies who surround me;
at his tabernacle will I sacrifice with
shouts of joy;
I will sing and make music to the Lord.
Psalms 27:1-6

PART ONE

LIVING IN THE CYCLE

1

McDonald's

I drove along the Garden State Parkway in New Jersey, headed for New York in a black, 1994 Jeep Cherokee, feeling so detached from myself while listening to the music coming out of the radio, or should I say, I was hearing the music, but not really listening. I couldn't really hear anything. I wasn't even sure if I was Lavon: the Lavon who portrayed the image of being so sure of herself in the face of any situation or the Lavon who smiled and laughed to cover up any imperfection in herself or family. Nothing about this Lavon felt real. I didn't know her, and I was scared—scared of what she might do; scared of the old self not being able to control it; and scared when every movement became a separate, intentional, entity of its own.

The gas pedal under my foot felt so alive, and my foot was willing itself to become a part of the pedal as I accelerated or slowed down. I thought if such a small, metal, square apparatus could have such power to determine the speed of my destination, why not join it. Then there were the blinkers: blink, blink, blink—willing my body to be a part of them; and the wipers—wissh, wissh, wissh; and the horn as well as the seats, the mirrors and the wheels on the car. Ahhhhh! You're losing it girl! Get a grip. It's gonna be all right. You'll feel like yourself soon enough. I promise. You'll get back control. Just don't bug out on me.

Oh God! I almost lost it there for a moment. If only I could have some connection, some link, my life would have meaning. Because at this point, everything I thought I was, wasn't holding true. Everything I thought I had was only an image of what I wanted it to be. I looked so intently at everything I touched and everything I passed as if that very thing could restore my life if I

15

willed myself to become a part of it, and I almost did. So, this is what a nervous breakdown must feel like.

When did it all go wrong? Where did it all go wrong? When did it all start?

It was Mommy's birthday, October 22, 1995, on a Sunday morning. I was standing in a McDonald's parking lot at a pay phone in Newburgh, New York. Only Marques and my mother knew I had left, but they didn't know exactly where I was. I had packed up two of my three children, leaving my oldest child, Marques with Herb.

I had had enough of Herb constantly threatening to kill me, carrying the bank books around with him in his black leather bag, telling me all the money was his, trying to control the friends I hung out with, and taking the Jeep during the summers I didn't work so I would have to stay home and away from my family.

The never ending cycle of verbal and emotional abuse over the last ten years just kept repeating itself and had finally taken it's toll on me, so I made the painful phone call home to Herb that went like this:

"Hi Herb."

"Lavon?"

"Yeah."

"Where are you?"

"I can't tell you that Herb. I left you."

"What!"

"I left, and I'm not coming back until you go get help and make some changes in your life because you always want to kill me and I'm afraid of you. I have Corey and Sheriah with me, and they are all right."

"Lavon, please don't do this! Please come back, and we'll talk about it."

"There's nothing to talk about Herb."

"Lavon, I'm sorry. I'm shaking all over. I was on my way to church with Marques. I'm shaking and can't stop."

"I'm sorry Herb. I'm really sorry."

"Lavon, please tell me where you are?"

"I can't do that."

"Please, Lavon! Please, Lavon!"

"Don't do this Herb. Please don't make this any harder for me than it already is. I gotta go. I'll call you later, bye."

Somehow, in the midst of all the confusion going on in my head and body, I was able to notice how the sun was high in the sky that morning creating a bright, clear, sunny day. Everything around me came together and engulfed all my senses, allowing me to observe the stillness of the moment. I wished to be a part of the whole scene and at peace with nature and myself. Cars were moving along looking more alive then I was. Even the streets with their thick, yellow lines going down the middle had a mystical quality about them. The streets looked like they could have been streets in New Jersey, except I wasn't in New Jersey anymore. I was in upstate New York.

People were in and out of McDonald's buying breakfast and doing what was natural for them. The flower arrangement surrounding McDonald's was so beautiful with its colored mixture of red, blue, yellow and purple flowers. The flowers looked so full of life that they had an acquiescent spirit about themselves that flowed with the natural order of things. And, here I was standing at a phone booth in a daze with tears running down my cheeks, looking at my two innocent children in the Jeep, who had no idea the course of their lives would be changed forever. They believed we were just out for a Sunday ride.

Even my children's normal behavior appeared abnormal to me. The noises they were making were as if I was hearing them for the first time. I tried to remember how many times I heard those silly, playful noises, in the hopes that the familiar noise would give me life. I needed to feel alive. I needed somebody, something to make me a part of its existence.

I walked back to my Jeep after hanging up the phone, not knowing exactly what I was going to do next or where I was going. I knew I had just made the scariest decision of my life. I kept trying to convince myself it was for the best and everything would work out—Herb would go get help; I would go back home; and we

would be a better, healthier family. It had to work out! It just *had* to!
My whole 'being' was depending upon it.

Nothing in the world could compare to the anguish I felt at
that moment. Where was the sense? Where was the connection?
What on earth was I doing standing in a McDonald's parking lot
with my two young children, not knowing a soul, being in a strange
land, thinking of going to a Battered Women's Shelter, and telling
my husband I had just left him? Explain this to me? Somebody,
please explain?

2

Realities

It was August. Herby and I had been separated for ten months now, and the separation was taking its toll on all of us, especially the kids. I couldn't afford to care for them financially. Herb offered no monetary support, and I didn't want our children split up anymore. With a heavy heart, I decided to let Corey and Sheriah live with their Dad and Marques for the next school year.

I spoke to Herb a few days later over the phone and expressed my concerns and intentions with him. Reluctantly, he conceded to allowing Corey and Sheriah to stay with him, and we agreed that I would come periodically to our home to help out.

A week before Labor Day, Herby and the kids came to my apartment in Newburgh to visit me and to discuss the arrangements for our children. My apartment was on the third floor of a three family brick building. I had a large bathroom the size of a young kid's room, a living room, kitchen and two bedrooms. My bedroom had a great view of the sun rising and setting over the Hudson River. The view compensated for the tattered, second hand furniture donated by the staff of the Battered Women's Shelter.

Herb and I were in my bedroom, sitting on my frameless bed talking, while our kids were down the hall in the living room, watching TV and playing. Herb's new plan was for the kids to stay with me, and he would help out financially. Even though I enjoyed seeing Herb and hearing our children laugh like old times, I told him I couldn't trust him, given his past history of not following through on the child support. So, we left things as planned and worked out what schools Corey and Sheriah would attend in New Jersey.

During our conversation, Herb made a statement that I'll never forget. We were talking about getting back together, but concluded that it wouldn't work because he didn't want to move to upstate New York, and I no longer wanted to live in New Jersey. I was trying to convince him that changes are good and sometimes necessary if we are to move forward in our lives. As I got up from the bed and started walking toward the dresser, Herby grumbled, "I would rather die first before making any changes in my life." That statement pierced right through my heart, stopping me dead in my tracks. I reached the dresser, leaned against it for support, and turned around to face Herby.

"Herb, please don't allow your fear to paralyze you to do nothing."

"I'm scared, Lavon."

"I know Herb. I'm scared, too. Because I love you, I will help you. But most importantly, God loves you and will help you make the changes if you just take the first step toward change."

"Lavon, I remember something you said to me, and I'll never forget it."

"What?"

"You said, we all have choices to make in our lives, and I'm choosing not to make any changes in my mine, even though I know you and God can help me."

"What are you afraid of Herb?"

"The unknown."

With tears in my eyes, I looked at my husband, who was 5 feet 8 inches tall and about 160 to 170 pounds. He had big, light brown pretty eyes with long curly eyelashes and a large nose. He had an oval shaped head with medium-size full lips, and his hair was cut close to his head, revealing waves. He was sitting on the edge of the bed with a drooped head and big sad eyes, looking so defeated by life, and I said, "Herb, you are right. We all have choices to make, and if that's your choice, I have to accept it, even though I'm sorry for the choice you have chosen for yourself. But, it's yours to make."

My heart was aching because, at that moment, I had finally lost my husband: the man I had fallen in love with; the man who had fathered my children; and the man I had spent sixteen years of my life with and struggled through ten years of marriage with. After all that, it now came down to the choices we make for ourselves.

Getting ready to leave, Herb stood up and said, "I love you, Lavon."

"I love you too, Herby."

He opened his arms for me as he stood at the front door. With hesitancy, I went into his arms, feeling like that would be my last time, and we hugged.

"Are you coming downstairs, Lavon?"

"No, not this time."

After I closed the door, I ran down the hallway in my apartment that led to my kitchen. I knelt down on the floor at the window to watch them leave. Herb was holding Sheriah's hand, crossing the street to go to his Jeep. I noticed his limp from a car accident had gotten worse. Tears began pouring down my cheeks like a waterfall because there was nothing I could do as a woman or mother to make our lives better. My heart and spirit sank for my family after Herb pulled off. I ran to my room and fell on my bed, crying like a baby, asking God to please help my husband and family.

On Saturday, September 7, 1996, two weeks after Herb and the kids visited me, I decided to pay them a surprise visit. The kids were going to start school on September 9, and I thought it would be a good idea for us to spend some time together and help Herby get them ready for school as I had promised.

My mother and sister, Andrea, drove from New Jersey to upstate New York to pick me up after work and bring me back to New Jersey (My Jeep had been repossessed). When we got into Jersey City, I dropped my mother off at work, taking her car and my sister to the house in Irvington.

I had discovered the first week of August that Herb was seeing another woman. She was from the church we all used to attend as a family. I wasn't sure if she would be at the house, but I knew it was a possibility. So, I informed my sister of what the situation might be, assuring her that I was all right and not to worry (Of course, I was worried though). I drove up the street, parked my mother's car in front of the house, got my bags out the trunk, walked up the porch steps with my sister and rang the bell. My oldest son, Marques, opened the door with a look of shock and surprise.

"Hi Marq," I said with a smile on my face as my sister, and I stepped in the house.

"Hi Ma. Hi Auntie Andrea."

Cheryl was sitting on my Victorian style white couch, talking on my phone. When she looked up and saw me, her face was more shocked and surprised than Marques' had been a minute ago. She hung up the phone. We said hello, and she asked Marq to beep his dad at work.

Corey and Sheriah helped overcome some of my hurt when they came running into my arms with smiles of happiness on their faces asking both at once; "Mommy, Mommy, are you staying?"

"Yeah."

"Yaaaa!" they yelled and began jumping up and down.

I took my bags up to my bedroom. I glanced around the room and noticed that it still looked the way I left it ten months ago. The papers and Bibles that I left on the dresser were still there, my jewelry box was in the same place with the jewelry I had left in it, and the same sheets were on the bed. Wow, this was scary!

Though everything appeared to be the same, something was vastly different—I no longer belonged. I was different. The furniture that I had once arranged in place couldn't make me belong, or the floral striped wallpaper that I looked at for nine years—even the blue carpet that my bare feet walked over millions of times didn't do it—and knowing that I laid side by side in the same bed with Herby and conceived two of our three children there couldn't do it.

I walked over to the side of the bed I used to sleep on and sat down, wondering how in the world was I going to get through four days in a house that didn't welcome me anymore. A house that was once full of laughter and love was now nothing but pain and bad memories. I told myself that it was for the sake of those smiling, young innocent faces downstairs.

With a renewed purpose, I gathered my composure and went back downstairs to the living room. Cheryl and Corey were sitting at the dining room table playing cards. My sister, Andrea, was sitting outside on the porch with Sheriah. I think Marques was in the kitchen. Before I could make my way to another room, the phone rang.

"Hello," I said.

"Hi, Lavon!"

It was Herb. As soon as I heard his voice, I headed upstairs with the cordless phone, thinking we were going to have a pleasant conversation.

"What are you doing there?"

"I came to visit and help get the kids ready for school."

"Well, I don't want you there."

"Why?"

"Let me speak to Marq."

"No, I want to talk to you."

"Let me speak to Cheryl."

"No. You are not talking to her either. Talk to me."

"I don't want to talk to you."

"Why? If you don't talk to me, then you won't talk to anybody."

"I'm coming home."

"You don't have to come home, I'm here now."

Herb hung up the phone on me, leaving me totally baffled and hurt by his hostile tone of voice and behavior. I had no clue why Herb responded so angrily towards me. So, I composed myself once again and went back downstairs as if nothing happened. I noticed Cheryl had gotten her things together and laid them by the side of the couch. She must have known I was talking to Herb. We were very cordial toward each other. She told me she had fixed dinner for my kids, and it was on the stove. I told her thank you.

Then, I went out on the porch where my sister and daughter were still sitting. I sat in the white, plastic chair that I always sat in and told my sister about the strange conversation I had with Herb. She asked me what was wrong with him, and I told her I really didn't know. I asked if she'd spend the night, and I'd take her home in the morning because Herb was on his way home and I didn't know if he would let me back in if I left. She said yeah and I sat back and prayed, asking God to grant me the serenity to accept the things I could not change and the courage to change the things I could, and the wisdom to know the difference.

After awhile, a white, Grand Cherokee Jeep drove up the street. It was Herb, and he looked pretty upset. I knew him well enough by his facial expressions to know when he was upset, even though I only got a quick glimpse of his face. It seemed as though our eyes locked as he drove past the house looking for a place to park. I watched him make a U-turn in the middle of the street a few houses down, park his Jeep on the same side of the street as our house, and get out.

My heart began beating faster as Herb approached the house. I told myself to stand my ground. Herb walked up the porch steps, spoke to Andrea in an easy tone of voice and looked at me as if he could kill me. Then, went right into the house.

As I look back on that day, the look on my husband's face should have been a sign to me that this wasn't the same Herb who had just come to my apartment two weeks ago and said, "I love you." But, I was tired of Herb's attitude. I was tired of being hurt. I was tired of being the one to leave when I did nothing wrong. I was tired and just didn't care anymore.

Anyway, Herb and I had made an agreement that I would come to the house and help him with the children. It made no sense to me why all of a sudden his attitude changed. That was his problem, and I wasn't leaving this time. Besides, my children were so happy to see me, and I was just as happy to see them. They were caught in the middle of so much of our troubles... There was no way I was going to disappoint them and take that happiness away.

I got up from the plastic chair I was sitting in on the porch and went into the house. Herb was sitting in the brown leather recliner that I bought him for our fifth wedding anniversary, which was under the arch between the living room and dining room. Cheryl was sitting on the edge of my couch, to the right of Herb, and I sat on my matching love seat, to the left of him.

"Why are you here, Lavon?"

"I told you I came to visit you and the kids and help them get ready for school, like we agreed."

"Well, Cheryl is here."

"Too bad. She'll just have to leave."

"She's not leaving."

"Oh yes she is!"

"We'll see."

"Yup, we'll see."

I sat there fuming and in disbelief as Herb got up from the recliner and went upstairs. Cheryl sat there, never saying a word. I knew there was no way I was going to let either of them know how hurt I really was, so I quickly resorted to a defensive posture and went upstairs to try and talk to Herb.

"Herb, what is going on? Why are you treating me like this?"

"Because I don't want you here. You abandoned the kids."

"Herb, what are you talking about? I didn't abandon the kids! I left them with you! You are their parent, too! Remember, this is what we agreed on."

"You did abandon the kids! I don't care what we agreed on!"

"Okay Herb, fine! Whatever you say. If that's what you think I did, then I guess I did. But I'm here now for four days to spend time with them and get'em ready for school, so why don't you just take Cheryl home and go on back to work."

"I'm not going back to work. This is my house! And maybe I want the both of you to stay with me."

"Well, that's just not going to happen! She's not staying here! What is wrong with you?"

All of a sudden Herb started grabbing at my breasts and butt. I was yelling for him to stop! But he wouldn't. His hands were all over me like he was an octopus. My mind started racing on how to get him off me. So I mushed him in the face, pushing him into the wall. He came at me and punched me in the stomach. I got him off me and ran downstairs with one shoe on to call the police. Herby ran after me and snatched the phone out of my hand, yelling that I couldn't use 'his' phone!

Cheryl was sitting in the recliner in the living room watching all this, and my sister, Andrea, was still sitting on the porch, unaware of what was happening. I ran out the house, still with one shoe on, past my sister and across the street to my neighbor Sylvia's house to call the police.

I stayed at Sylvia's house until the cops arrived. We sat out on the enclosed porch talking when I saw the police drive up in front of my house. Before they could get out of their car, I walked over to my house and waited on the porch for them with Andrea, Corey, and Sheriah.

They had on their dark blue uniforms and shiny black shoes. Both officers were men, and both were black. Herb and Cheryl were in the kitchen, I think, when the police and I entered the house. The police asked, "Who called?"

"I did," I said.

At some point, Herb and Cheryl came into the living room when one of the officers asked me what happened.

I said, "My husband and I have been separated for ten months because he was abusing me. I came to visit and help him get our children ready for school because that's what we agreed on two weeks ago at my apartment in Newburgh. I am not leaving because this is still my house. When I went upstairs to talk to my husband, he started attacking me sexually, and I slapped him and mushed him in the face, pushing him into the wall. Then he came at me and punched me in my stomach."

Herby told them he didn't attack me or punch me in the stomach. It came down to my word over his word and who the police were going to believe.

I was leaning against the arm of my couch with my arms folded across my chest, looking very defiant. Herb was sitting on the arm of the love seat. We were both facing the police officers, which were standing closest to me, next to the door and stairs. Cheryl was still sitting in the recliner.

The shorter officer asked Herb if we had made an agreement, and Herb said, "No!" This shocked them and me. I could tell from the way things were going and the looks of their faces that they were confused and didn't know how to quite handle the situation.

"Wait a minute, wait a minute! Whose house is this?" The shorter officer said.

"Mine!" Herby and I both said together.

"Okay then. Who lives here?" asked the Officer.

"I do. She hasn't lived here in ten months." Herb said.

"So what! It's still my house!

"Well, where do you live?" the Officer asked.

"I live upstate New York."

"Well, who is she?" one of the officers asked.

"That's my husband's girlfriend!"

The police looked at Herb, then at each other and dropped their heads. Things were getting worse by the minute, but they were still trying to make sense out of all this. The taller officer spoke first. He turned toward me and said, "Well, what do you expect? You've been gone all this time, what was he suppose to do?"

I looked at him with a blaze of fire in my eyes. Before I could retort, the smaller officer stepped in and suggested that everybody cool down. He decided that in order to try and gain some understanding of the situation and come to a solution, one of them would take me outside on the porch to get my side of the story while the other talked with Herb in the house.

The tall officer and I both walked out on the porch, and he said, "Okay, tell me your story."

With my hands on my hips, an attitude in my voice, I said, "I left my husband and no longer live here because in October of 1995, he threatened to kill me. I moved to upstate New York and was living in a Battered Women's Shelter for awhile. From June of 1996 until now, my husband would come to New York with our children and visit me. We got along fine, and I'm not afraid of him anymore and don't believe he will try and kill me, but as far as us living together as husband and wife we just can't work things out. Two weeks ago in my apartment, we made an agreement that all the children would stay with him, and I would come into town from time to time and help him until I get on my feet financially. Then, our children will come and live with me." I also told the officer that this was my house and under no circumstances was he putting me out! I walked back into the house.

He then took Cheryl outside to speak with her (for what I don't know). They were out there for about five minutes while I waited inside the house with Herby and the shorter officer. The officer was still talking to Herby in a low whisper, and Herb was nodding his head up and down.

After all the talking was done, the shorter officer took charge again and concluded that Cheryl had to leave and that I could stay and try to work things out with Herby. (What the officer didn't realize was that by this time, I no longer wanted to work anything out with Herb. I was only staying because of my children, but I was glad he told Herb that Cheryl had to leave.) The officer also let Herb and I both know that if they had to come back for any reason, one of us would be arrested. Shortly after that, they left.

3

The Shooting

I returned to Sylvia's house in total disbelief of Herb's behavior to wait until Cheryl left. I told Sylvia that I had the illusion when I planned the visit that Herb would be glad to see me. I thought he would just take Cheryl home, and we all would have a good time together as a family. It never occurred to me that I was just fantasizing and Herby would do a flip-flop on me like that—but I guess he had to show time in front of his girlfriend, and lord knows what he was telling her.

After awhile, I called my Pastor, Reverend Lewis, in Newburgh, from Sylvia's house and told him what happened. I expressed some fear about staying at the house with Herb. Because of my faith in God, he assured me everything would be all right and that God had a great plan for me and didn't want me yet. When I saw Cheryl come out of my house and get into a car, I thanked Sylvia for all her help and support and returned home. Herb was talking to my sister in the living room about the Book Publishing Company they used to work at together, as if nothing had happened. I sat at the other end of the couch, never saying a word to him. Our children were sitting on the living room floor watching television. Things seemed to have calmed down, and everybody was trying to settle in for the night.

Later, I got all three of my children ready for bed because we were going to have a busy day, starting first thing the next morning. I told them I loved them and how sorry I was for everything that happened and that tomorrow would be better. I kissed them all goodnight and went into the bathroom. Breaking down and crying, I prayed, asking God once again to please help my family and me

29

so we could move to a better phase of our lives. I also asked God to release me from my marriage (for the hundredth time), but to help Herb and me to get along in order to be better parents to our children. Then, I went into my bedroom and changed the sheets with the sheets I had brought with me from my apartment in Newburgh. (Even though I had paid for the sheet on the bed, there was no way I was going to sleep on the same sheet Herb and his woman had slept on. It was bad enough that I was sleeping in the bed.)

I sat on the bed, praying to hold on to my faith. I took my clothes off and put on my white, red and black long Snoopy nightshirt. Before I got in bed, I checked on my sister downstairs. She was fast asleep in the recliner. I got a blanket, put it on her and went back upstairs. I climbed in my bed for the first time in ten months, hoping that when I lay down, sleep would overtake me too. Herb was fuddling around in the bathroom and came to bed a while later.

Sometime during the night I heard noise coming from downstairs. I got out of the bed and walked down the steps and saw that the television was on. Marques was up watching the Apollo. I sat down on the couch with him and asked if he was all right. He said, "Yeah. I just can't sleep, Ma."

When a commercial came on, he turned to me and said real serious and in a low voice, "Ma, I have to tell you something about Daddy?"

"What is it, Marq?" I said still half asleep.

"Daddy is different. He's not the same."

"What you mean, Daddy is different? Different how?"

"I think something's wrong with Daddy—and I'm afraid of him."

"Why are you afraid of him? Tell me what's been going on."

Before Marques could respond, we heard someone walking down the stairs. It was Herb. He came and stood a few feet away from us in his underwear and tee shirt and asked Marques why was he afraid of him. Marques froze. I watched his face turned pale black, his eyes widen and his whole body stiffened. I looked from

Marq to Herb and back to Marq again, and still, Marques didn't say a word. He just sat there wide-eyed, staring at his dad. The only other sound in the room beside the TV was my sister Andrea's snoring. Finally, without pressing the issue any further, Herby walked away without saying a word or showing any kind of anger and went back upstairs. Color returned to Marques' skin, and he set back against the couch. I asked him if he was okay, and he shook his head yes, but I wasn't so sure. I rubbed his head, telling him we would talk later at my apartment. We finished watching the rest of the Apollo before going back upstairs to bed.

The next morning I was up by 6:30 a.m. I was going to take my sister home to Jersey City and pick my mother up from work. When we got in the car, I told Andrea about Marques' shocking statement to me about being afraid of his dad and his fearful reaction to Herb when he came downstairs.

"Vonny, I think Herb's buggin' out. He looked so crazy yesterday and Marques probably sees him acting weird."

"I know. I don't know what's wrong with Herb, but I might have to bring the kids to live with me now—money or no money." We drove the rest of the way in silence.

An hour and a half later, I returned home and everybody was still asleep. I was really grateful that my sister's presence helped me get through the night. I climbed into the bed again hoping to fall back asleep. After a half an hour or more passed and I still wasn't asleep, I decided it was time to get up and get started.

My plan was to bring my children to Newburgh so we could attend the 3:00 p.m. service at church and spend time together at my apartment so I could talk to Marques about his dad. Then, I would drive back to New Jersey, get the kids clothes ready for school—have them take their baths and settle them down for bed—and finally relax.

I woke Marques up first to take his bath that morning. He asked where his Auntie Andrea was, and I told him I took her home. He went into this panic screaming, "You shouldn't have done that, Ma! Why did you take her home?"

I didn't understand his panic so I told him to calm down; it'd be all right. He just kept saying, "You shouldn't have done that. You shouldn't have done that." Before I left his room, I asked him in a concerned voice why I shouldn't have done that? He just said, "Forget it, Ma."

My mind was on so many other things, such as getting the kids washed and dressed so that they would have enough time to eat breakfast before we left, that I didn't have time to give Marques' strange reaction too much thought. I just told myself that I would call Rev when I got home and tell him about Marques' fear of his dad and the panic he showed when I told him that I took my sister home. Hopefully he would come up with an explanation.

I got Corey in the tub next. After he got dressed, he and Marques went down to the basement to watch TV. It was about 9:00 a.m. when I ran Sheriah's bath water. I was on schedule in order to be out of the house by 11:00 a.m. I had to wash Sheriah's hair and braid it, get her dressed and then get myself together.

Herb was just waking up by the time I put Sheriah in the tub. She wanted to stay in the tub awhile before I washed her hair. Herb came into the bathroom as I was coming out. He had on his underwear and the yellow tank top I always remembered him wearing. It was almost like old times. He spoke to me very lovingly—calling me Babe. He sounded like the Herb I knew and fell in love with. For a minute, I thought maybe there was still a chance that we could work things out, but then I quickly reminded myself of the night before. Sheriah yelled out, "Hey Daddy," and he started playing with her and then went downstairs.

The phone rang while I was in the bedroom waiting for my daughter to finish playing in the tub. It was for Herb. I went back into the bathroom to start washing Sheriah's hair. It was really dirty. I had to wash it three or four times. I don't think anyone had washed it since I last washed it in June, and now it was September. I felt bad about that. I washed her up afterwards—took her out of the tub and dried her off. She put her panties on, I wrapped her in a big pink towel, and we went downstairs. Herb was in the dining room, still on the phone in his underwear and yellow tank top. He sounded agitated. The conversation was centered on the night before. Marques and Corey were in the living room with their shorts and tee shirts on. They were sitting on the couch watching Bobby Jones' Gospel. I sat in the recliner with Sheriah between my legs so I could begin braiding her hair. As I began combing Sheriah's hair out, I heard Herb say to the person on the phone that he wanted to have a family meeting. As he was hanging up, he apparently decided that's what we would have.

"Lavon," he stated in a matter of fact tone, "I want a family meeting."

"I'm not having a family meeting, Herb." (I couldn't believe after what happened last night with Cheryl that he thought I was going to have a family meeting with him and the kids.)

"Why?"

"Because I don't want to."

Herby walked over to where I was sitting. He got real close to my ear and yelled as loud as he could in the strangest voice that I ever heard, *"This—is—my—house!"* His mouth was opened real wide. Small splotches of spit got on my face, and he was drooling at the mouth. Marques and Corey jumped off the couch while Sheriah and I practically leaped out of the recliner. We all stood there in the middle of the floor holding on to each other, looking at Herb as if he were a monster. His eyes were bulging and very glassy.

"This is why Mommy can't come back here and live," I blurted out to my kids; who along with me were very scared and confused.

Herb then walked past us and went up the stairs as if nothing happened. After he was gone, we all resumed our seats, but I felt very uneasy as I went back to combing out Sheriah's hair. Bobby Jones' credits were going up the television screen when a thought came to me to change my plans and speed them up. Instead of having the kids get dressed for church here, I decided I would have them bring their clothes with them to Newburgh and get dressed at my apartment. I would put on the same clothes from yesterday and take my shower when I got to my apartment. I would no longer cornrow Sheriah's hair, but I would put two or three ponytails in it (depending on the amount of barrettes I could find) until we got to my apartment.

I got up from the recliner to go upstairs to look for some barrettes. I was still in my white, red, black, Snoopy nightshirt and slippers. The kids were all downstairs in the living room waiting. When I reached the last three steps from the top, Herby was standing there to the side so I could pass because our staircase is narrow and steep. He was dressed in his clothes from the day before, black jeans and a gray tee shirt. I thought this odd because he had already ironed his clothes for church, but I kept moving toward our bedroom.

I climbed up on the bed, having to stand on my tippy-toes so I could see over the tall, brown armoire for barrettes, when Herb came into the room.

"Lavon, I want to talk to you!"

"I don't want to talk, Herb."

I eased myself off the bed, moving to the lower dresser still searching for barrettes, when Herb repeated again that he wanted to talk. And again, I said, "No."

"Are you going to talk to me now?"

Herb was standing to the side of me. I turned my head toward him to see what he was talking about. I looked directly down the black barrel of a gun. The gun was pointing straight at my left temple.

"*Herb, no!*" Was all that I could say in a voice so meek that it sounded like it belonged to a little girl instead of a grown woman and mother of three. I barely got the words out of my mouth when the blast from the gun filled the room.

He shot me! Oh my God! He shot me! I'm dying! I'm standing here dying! The blackness of death is overtaking my life. Slowly, slowly, slowly, the shadowy Blackness is moving through the left side of my body. The bullet of death has entered my head with such a forceful blast that it slows everything down—even death. The Blackness is like no other blackness I've ever seen. It's different from the night darkness I've grown accustomed to. The Blackness has a life and color of its own. It comes to claim. To claim what's rightfully been given over—Life.

The Blackness moves within a grayish white shadowy mist, ever so slowly—so sure of its claim—so full of life. Moving with the assurance of another victim. With no thought of innocence or guilt—no respect of race, color, creed, gender, mother, father, brother, sister, daughter, son, status.

The woman diving down a flight of fifteen stairs dodging bullets, can't be the same woman who ran upstairs, past her husband looking for barrettes. How could this be? The woman who ran upstairs knew she was a mother, wife, sister, daughter, friend, strong, courageous, sad, happy, lonely. The woman diving down the stairs knew she had a bullet in her head and knew she was going to die any minute, but had no clue who she was. The woman knew she had to be one in the same person, sharing the same body. The woman diving down the stairs didn't know her. This wasn't part of her make-up. This scene didn't fit the script. The woman who ran upstairs was only interested in looking for barrettes, not hearing six gunshots ring out all around her. The woman looking for the barrettes instantly turned into the woman looking down a dark, small black hole of the barrel of a gun. How could this be? The same person playing different roles of her self only happens in the movies or on TV, not in the privacy of her own home, standing in her bedroom next to her husband of ten years. She wasn't prepared for this new role. There wasn't any training involved, but that didn't stop the scene from being played out. It took on a life of its own.

Not fair! Not fair! The woman wanted out. She didn't like how the script was written, or how the blast from the gunshot hung in the air, or the burning sensation she felt in her head, giving further evidence she was shot. She didn't like the stillness of the moment, or the way the blackness was overtaking her body with each movement of the bullet through her head that could leave her lifeless, or not knowing what to do next. How could this be? Feeling the ping of something in her butt and hearing herself saying, "Woo, where did that come from?" What kind of script is this anyway? People saying woo when they are being shot at. She almost laughed and thought yeah, this must be a joke, a horrible, horrible joke no one told her about until she realized that the ping she felt was a bullet.

Oh Lord! What to do next? Before she could think her arms were outstretched, and she was literally diving from the top of the stairs from a standing position. Those stairs didn't feel like the same stairs she had just run up five minutes ago. How could this be?

When she opened her eyes, she saw she was half way down the stairs with her left hand holding the left side of her head from the excruciating pressure, using her right arm to pull her body forward and kicking off with the back of her feet like a swimmer would do (Oh, they want me to swim! I can do that).

She's screaming the names of her children, "Marques! Corey! Sheriah!" like a crazy woman now, because the two women merge into one for the love of the children. How and when did she remember she had children? When did she become the whole of the woman being shot at and the woman looking for barrettes? And why are bullets being fired at me? Now it's personal. It's me, not she any more. What next?

When I got to the bottom of the stairs, I crawled around the banister into the living room—jumping up from the floor and yelling for my children to come to me. Terrified and huddled close together, my children and I ran to the kitchen, where the back door was located—not knowing where Herby was.

Marques flung the chain off the door—unlocked it—and pulled it opened with all his strength. We all ran out the door onto the gray, wooden porch, down the steps, to the long, black, asphalt driveway. As we ran toward the street, I screamed over and over, "Someone help me! Someone help me!"

We were headed for my neighbor's house across the street, but before I got fully to the other side, something within me caused me to look back. *Oh my God!* Standing under a large oak tree in front of our house with just her panties on, a pink towel stretched across her back and her hair dripping wet, was my four-year-old daughter, Sheriah. *Oh God! She didn't run! I have to go back for her!*

At that moment, the whole universe seemed to open up and become very still and peaceful. It was as if God had stopped the world, phased everything out to insure my safety. There were no cars driving down the street. The sky was the clearest blue I had ever seen with huge white clouds that looked like thick balls of cotton I could float on. I fought back my fear and ran to my daughter, grabbing her by the hand and dragging her across the street to where Marques and Corey were nervously waiting.

Once across the street, we all started running again toward my neighbor's house. Marques got to the door first, ringing the bell without stopping until somebody opened the door. We flew in the house not knowing who opened the door. I was yelling, "Herby shot me! Herby shot me!" and then began crawling through the living room and dining room toward the kitchen. I heard the panic of screaming female voices coming from the front of the house, but I continued crawling, praying that I wouldn't die and feeling sorry for Sylvia and her daughters because there was nothing I could do to calm the women's nerves.

Joyce, my neighbor's daughter, walked beside me the whole time crying and begging for me to lie down. I cried, "I don't want my blood to mess up the carpet!" After reaching the kitchen, I lay down on the hard, marble-looking tile floor. I was in between the doorway of the kitchen and dining room. The stove, refrigerator and counter top were to the right of me, and the built in china cabinet and bathroom were at my left.

Joyce was still at my side, sitting on the floor next to me, crying hysterically. I tried consoling her by telling her that I was all right. But after turning my head slightly to the left and seeing a pool of my blood on the floor, I wasn't so sure. I didn't go into a panic like I wanted too. I just turned my head and laid my hair in the blood to soak some of it up. The stove was on, and the weather was very warm for the month of September, adding to the extremely hot temperature in the kitchen. Sweat was running into my eyes, stinging them, but I was too afraid to move. My mind was telling me I was supposed to be dead, and Joyce sounded like she was about to go into shock any minute. I didn't know which was worse, giving into the soothing blackness of death or fighting to stay alive and remain in the unbearable situation. I was tired; really tired.

In the midst of the chaos and trying to stay alive, Sylvia walked into the kitchen. I asked her to please pray with me. I was so scared that I didn't know what else to do. Sylvia was in no shape to pray or do anything else for that matter, though, and probably thought I was crazy. We didn't pray so I prayed by myself, thanking God for all He had done for me and asking Him for His help. Actually, I wanted to change places with Sylvia for a few minutes to help calm her down, and her two daughters. I figured since I was the cause of all the panic and I didn't know how to be a victim, I could at least lend some assistance. I did manage to get Sylvia's attention again to give her the phone numbers of my mother, my Pastor, and Herb's sister, Bertha, so she could call and tell them what happened. I also told her to keep my children downstairs in the basement so they wouldn't see all the chaos and the blood on the floor. By this time, two police officers had rushed into the house. They were trying to calm everybody down in order to find out what happened. A young, good looking, bald headed black police officer that I knew came into the kitchen. He rushed right over to where I was, dressed in his neat, tight, dark blue uniform. He asked, "Did your husband shoot you in the head?" After hearing my muffled response, he patted me softly on the back. A few seconds passed, and he was gone.

Five or ten minutes later, I heard squeals of crying coming from the front enclosed porch. They sounded like cries of death. For some reason, I knew then that my husband had shot and killed himself. A few minutes later, the same good-looking officer came back into the kitchen to check on me. I asked him if my husband shot himself and where? With a look of surprise on his face, he said, "Yes, in the head, but he's not dead." I thanked him and prayed to God for my husband's spirit and my life.

The house was beginning to get full and started looking like a crime scene that you see on TV. The paramedics had arrived, more police officers were there, and neighbors had gathered outside. I could hear all the commotion going on inside and outside of my head. Sylvia was talking to the police. Her other daughter, Moni, was crying and talking. Different police officers and paramedics were across the street at my house attending to my husband. Rob, one of my neighbors, kept running back and forth checking on my husband and me, keeping me informed of his condition and encouraging me to hang in there. There were voices coming over the police and paramedics radios. People were crying and I wasn't exactly sure where my children were. They were the only ones I didn't see.

I was motionless on the kitchen floor with Joyce still at my side, crying hysterically, and the police and paramedics standing over me. They were all talking to each other trying to determine the extent of my injuries. They saw all the blood on the floor from my head, but they couldn't locate the bullet wound because the blood was matted to my hair. After a few minutes of searching through my hair, the black woman paramedic found the entry wound. The fact that she was a woman and was black relieved some of my internal fears. She had a warm, friendly face that communicated to me that I was safe and she wasn't going to let anything else happen to me. But, I couldn't understand why the other police and paramedics had concerned looks on their faces and why they were examining other parts of my body when they had already found the bullet wound. They were all looking at my foot, talking very low when I asked if I could have a pillow to rest my foot because it was really hurting. They all looked up at me and said, "No! Your foot can't be elevated." I didn't understand why the sharp tones and started to get angry, but the pressure in my head and neck increased slightly, causing me to think otherwise.

Now they were looking down at my nightgown, pointing at something around my behind. I could see them out of the corner of my right eye. One of the officers started lifting my nightgown and I yelled out, "What are you doing? You can't do that! I have nothing on!" (Talking about wearing clean underwear in case of an accident! Oh well.) The Officer was very nice about it and said he was sorry, but they had to check because it looked like I had another gunshot wound.

I said, "Okay, but please don't look."

They all agreed and laughed. I was so embarrassed that I tried thinking about something else while they looked at my big, black butt. It was confirmed. I was shot in the butt! A part of me wanted to laugh, but I heard them saying, I was shot in my left foot, too. My mind started racing, going over the facts. There was a bullet in my head—another in my butt, and one more in my foot. Something's not right—that's three bullets! I've been shot three times! When? How? I didn't feel them. I only knew about the one in my head—the first one, when Herby pointed the gun and pulled the trigger. How can I be alive after being shot three times?

As the reality of my condition sank in, the fear of my dying became greater. The internal struggle going on inside of me grew. My mind kept saying, "I should be dead," but my spirit kept saying, "Uh uh." In order to relax, I prayed to God for my spirit to be drawn closer into His presence.

While still lying on the kitchen floor, the paramedics placed a big, white, dog collar of a brace around my neck to stabilize my head. Next, they rolled me onto a long, narrow, brown, hard board. I was flat on my back when one of the officers noticed blood on the front of my nightgown. They lifted my gown once again and there was another gunshot wound in my upper, left thigh. *Oh Lord, four bullets! Herby shot me four times!*

Being a claustrophobic, my fear increased because of the brace around my neck, and being so confined to the board. I continued to relinquish my spirit to the presence of God, hoping to get through the whole, unbelievable ordeal. I was strapped to the board and lifted from the kitchen floor by the police and paramedics. There were small slots around the edge of the board for them to put their fingers through. They carried me out the front door and down the steps to the waiting ambulance, where a crowd had gathered. I shut my eyes, trying not to cry and prayed that they wouldn't drop me. I already had the worst headache of my life.

4

ER

In the ambulance, Dena, the black woman paramedic, tried to administer oxygen by placing a clear green oxygen mask over my nose and mouth. But, I rocked from side to side in shear panic, gasping for breath, begging her to take the mask off. She finally did, and then I breathlessly explained to her that I am claustrophobic. She calmed me down by talking to me softly and rubbing my shoulder, assuring me she wouldn't put the mask back on. I relaxed the best I could after that.

That was my second time in an ambulance. The first time was when my son Marques had a seizure and had to be rushed to the hospital. I was in a state of panic then, too. I don't remember any smells or seeing much equipment either time. What I do remember was how boxed shaped and cramped the space was in the back of the ambulance. Ironically, I was grateful for the closeness the second time in the ambulance because of the peace of mind it gave me.

Dena could see how sleepy I was becoming and urged me not to go to sleep. She held my hand the whole time, which was very comforting to me. We prayed and talked about how good God is. When we arrived at the hospital, I thanked her for all she had done for me.

Doctors and nurses were in white and green gowns with stethoscopes around their necks, moving with such urgency. I could only see right in front of me the rush of doctors desperately trying to examine me after I was rolled into a room. I could hear the rustling of the doctors' feet, the excitement and loudness of their voices, the panicked silence in their eyes. I heard a stretcher being rolled down the hall past my room and managed to see it was some other paramedics rolling my husband into an emergency room next to mine.

The whole scene was just like the TV series ER. Police were in my room questioning me about the shooting. I heard them place my husband under arrest for attempted murder. A policeman was guarding his door. They also placed the yellow tape with black writing on it that's used in a crime scene, around his door as a barrier. It was amazing watching and hearing all the action, with me being the center of attention.

The doctors reminded me of buzzing, busy bees who had just discovered the greatest tasting honey as they hovered over me with looks of excitement, disbelief and readiness. But, at the same time they had stern *looks* of well-educated white men that said, "We know it all."

Once again, I had to submit to the whole ordeal of being probed and poked. I lay there and prayed for it all to be over with soon. I think there were about four of them trying to find the gunshot wound to my head. It felt like all forty fingers were in my hair at the same time. I just wanted them to hurry up and go about their business.

The 'Buzzing Busy Bees' finally found the entry wound in the back of my skull, but they couldn't locate the bullet.

"Did it exit?"

"No, it's not there."

"Is it over here, you think?"

Oh lord, are they for real? Of course the bullet didn't exit dummies (I wanted to say), *it's on the other side of my head.*

I realized the doctors were going to keep searching so I called to my nurse Gina, who seemed to be about my age or a little older and told her where the bullet was and asked her if she would please tell somebody. I figured since they didn't ask me, I shouldn't be the one to tell them, even though it was my head. My nurse spoke very slowly and calmly because the doctors were still attacking like bees in pursuit of honey.

"Doctors. Doctors. The patient said the bullet isn't over there. It's on the right side of her head."

They all looked up as if she said we had discovered a cure for cancer. In unison, the four buzzing busy bees appeared to be on their tippee-toes, scurrying over to the right side of my bed with their hands stretched out, going for the prize.

Oh lord, not again! Those same forty fingers probed and poked the right side of my head as they did the left.

"She's right! Here it is!" (As if I could have been wrong, I thought to myself.)

The room filled with more buzzing excitement as each doctor felt the bullet for himself to confirm the first doctor's find. Their voices had a tone of disbelief that the bullet actually did pass through to the other side of my head and yet I wasn't dead and there wasn't anything visibly wrong with me. There was also a questioning tone that rang out in their voices. It wasn't until the neuro-surgeon examined me that I understood the questioning tone in their voices. They never spoke to me, not even to say thank you. They got their taste of honey and cheap thrills from my body and scampered out of the room together to God knows where.

I thought about my husband over in the next room. He was on life support, and I really wanted to see him. His nurse came over to my room and informed me of his condition. He shot himself once in the head, shattering his brain and wasn't expected to live. *He really did it. He really tried to kill me and commit suicide.*

Everything happened so suddenly. One minute I was looking for barrettes and the next minute I was looking down the barrel of a gun, running for my life with four bullets in me. It just didn't seem possible. Lying on the stretcher, I wondered what all that meant to me. All my emotions were numb. I wasn't sure of anything. *Did the shooting really happen or did I dream it all? Was that me swimming down the stairs trying to dodge bullets, running out of the house with my three children screaming? Was that us? Was that Herb shooting at me? Is this me lying on the stretcher in the emergency room of University Hospital and my husband in the next room on life support about to die?* I thought maybe if I saw Herby reality would click in.

There was no time to wait on reality though because another doctor walked in, a different one. Everything about him was different from the "Buzzing Busy Bees." This doctor was about business. It showed in his experience as he confidently parted my matted bloody hair. He knew exactly what exams he was going to perform.

Dressed in rather spiffy, casual clothes, it looked like he was out having brunch or something. He was of average height and had a slender build and looked to be about in his mid-forties (with a well-groomed, salt and pepper beard.)

I kept wondering what kind of doctor he was. No one introduced him to me or talked to me yet. All the doctors would just come in and start performing their examinations on me without even a "Hi, I'm so and so and this is the reason I'm here." This Doctor was a lot more relaxed and friendly, though. Eventually, he had to talk to me because the kind of exams he did required some answers.

I had no clue at the time why he examined my head, neck and ears. He looked at the back of the right and left side of my head, feeling with the tips of his fingers on the right where he located the bullet. He felt around the spine of my neck. He snapped his fingers close to both of my ears twice, asking me if I could hear. I told him the sound to my right ear was clear, but the sound to my left ear was a little faint.

He checked me over one last time and said to the doctors standing at the head of my bed, waiting eagerly for his results, "There's nothing wrong with this patient. The bullet is lodged in the fat tissues of her neck. Her spinal and vocal cords have not been damaged, her hearing is all right and she's not paralyzed. She doesn't need surgery, and the bullet can stay in her neck until it surfaces."

Then, he left.

For the first time I realized the severity of the bullet passing from one side of my head to the other. I looked up at my nurse, who was now standing on the right side of my bed, holding my hand. She looked down at me, and we both smiled as she squeezed my hand slightly and tears rolled down the side of my face.

Hallelujah! Thank God! I am not going to die! I was fine. At least, I was not going to die this day from the bullet in my head, and I didn't need surgery. *Yes!* The other three bullets didn't seem to be posing any life-threatening danger. All I wanted after that was to be sent home with some Tylenol for my headache. How blessed could a person be?

At that time, I thought that would be the end of it and I'd get to go home, but the next thing I knew hospital attendants were wheeling me down the hall to have an MRI. The top half of my body would be inside of this huge, white, circular shaped machine taking x-rays of my head. They had to place an IV in my arm that had a certain kind of dye in it that would highlight the bullet in my head. Gina could see the fear in my eyes when she explained the procedure to me. She asked what was wrong, and I told her that I was a claustrophobic and couldn't go in that machine. She said it was necessary, but promised she'd be by my side the whole time.

Unfortunately, they didn't put the IV in my arm properly, and all the dye ran out all over me while I was in the machine. I had to go through the entire nightmare again.

From there, I was rolled down the hall into another x-ray room. This room was not as bright or modern as the room I had just come out. The other room was full of sophisticated, technological machinery. This room was old, drab and dull with a stale smell. When I was placed on the long, slab, x-ray table, it was hard and cold. It looked like it came right out of a Frankenstein movie.

The attendants x-rayed my foot, thigh, and buttocks, all while the neck brace was on and I was still lying on the hard board. I don't remember how the attendants managed to take the x-rays, but I do remember being very uncomfortable and finding it difficult to lie still for all those x-rays.

Three more nameless doctors entered the room through a back door. They hovered over in a corner a little ways away from me talking and inspecting my x-rays. They didn't realize that I could hear some of what they were saying. I thought I heard something about surgery and internal bleeding. *Oh, please let me be wrong!*

I called my nurse over to me when she came back into the room. I told her what I thought I had heard and asked her if it was true. She said she'd find out. I also asked her to please tell the doctors to come and speak to me about my condition since I could hear them discussing me. I don't remember if they did because I had to go to the bathroom really bad at that moment. Gina helped me on to the bedpan while the doctors looked on curiously.

"Gina, I can't go. Nothing won't come out. It's right there. I feel it. Why can't I pee?"

"It's all right, honey. I have to catheterize you."

"Will it hurt?"

"Maybe a little. The doctors think you may be bleeding internally. The bullet from your buttocks went into your stomach, and they can't locate it on the x-ray. They think it may be in your intestines, and that's why you can't go to the bathroom."

"Are they going to have to operate?" I asked in a whiney voice.

"I don't know. If blood doesn't come out when you urinate, maybe not."

Oh God, please don't let blood come out! Gina placed this long, yellowish, thin tube in my urethra, though I didn't know what it was called at the time. Immediately, the pee came gushing down the tube. *Oh, what a relief!*

"Is there any blood, Gina?"

"No."

"No surgery, right!"

Gina glanced over at the doctors (who were still in the corner watching) and said she didn't know. She knew I was upset and afraid so she went and got my mother, who was in the waiting room with my sisters, brother, aunts and uncles.

My mother came into the x-ray room, and I told her the doctors were thinking about doing surgery to find the bullet in my stomach. I also told her I was *not* having surgery. Then I started crying. She stroked my face and told me to calm down, that it'd be

46

all right. She stayed with me when they rolled me back to the emergency room. It was about 3:00 in the afternoon by then.

For the first time that day, a doctor actually came over to talk to me. He introduced himself as Doctor so and so and said with a determined voice, "Mrs. Grant, we believe the bullet is lodged somewhere around your spleen, colon or intestines, and it has to be removed. So, therefore, we decided that you will need surgery even though there isn't any blood present in your urine. I'll be the doctor performing the surgery."

As he handed me the clipboard with the consent forms, I informed him that I was not having surgery, nor did I care where the bullet was located and wouldn't sign the forms. He stared at me wondering if I was serious, then at my mother who was standing at the side of my bed, hoping she could change my mind.

"Vonny, you gotta have the surgery."

"No I don't, Ma. It's gonna hurt, and I don't want them cutting me."

The doctor walked over to the other doctors, obviously frustrated. I didn't care. A good-looking young doctor then came over to me telling me it was illegal to leave bullets in the stomach.

"Too bad. I'm not having surgery."

"You have to have the surgery."

"No I don't. And I'm not."

"Mom," he pleaded, " please talk to her."

I shook my head. He walked back over to the doctors just as exasperated as the first. My mother asked why I wouldn't have the surgery. I told her because I was scared. The first doctor came back over to me with a stern tone of voice, badgering me again about having surgery. I couldn't fight them anymore so I closed my eyes and said a quick prayer to God. "God, please tell me what to do!"

"I'll never leave you, nor forsake you," I heard someone say.

I opened my eyes and said, "Okay, I'll have the surgery. But understand, it's God performing the surgery through you."

The doctor looked totally stunned, but he quickly regained his composure. He yelled, startling the team of doctors, "Get things set up!"

He explained to my mother and me that the surgery would be exploratory because they weren't certain where the bullet was lodged. My mind was rushing a mile a minute, and out of the blue, I asked, "Since you have to cut me, can you please tie my tubes?"

The doctor's face turned beet red as he, my nurse and mother broke out in laughter; causing me to laugh myself out of one pain and into the next. Except, I wasn't trying to be funny. I was serious.

He said, "I can't do that."

"Okay then, can you remove some of the fat?"

This time we could not control our laughter as well as we did before. He did manage to say though, "We don't do that either!"

The laughter relieved most of the tension in the room. Rapidly, the doctor started prepping me for surgery as if I was going to change my mind. The nurses removed me from the hard board. They took my blood pressure and checked my heart rate. Someone called upstairs to let them know I was on my way. Just before leaving the emergency room, the doctor finally had Gina remove the neck brace.

The last thing I remember before they performed surgery was fighting with a doctor who was trying to put an oxygen mask over my face. He placed the mask on, and I pulled it up, trying to explain to him that I was claustrophobic. He put it back on, holding it firmly down on my face and said, "You have to leave on the mask!" I said, "No I don't!" and pulled it off again. We went back and forth like that a few more times until a big, fat, short, white doctor saw us and came over. He patted the younger doctor or intern on the shoulder and said in a controlled soft voice, "Leave her alone. She'll soon be unconscious from the anesthesia. Then you can place the mask on her."

When he turned to leave I licked my tongue out at the doctor standing over my head and closed my eyes and started counting, 10, 9, 8... Sure enough, less then ten seconds of the incident I was in la-la land.

Through it all, my greatest challenge was fighting for my life by staying conscious. Everyone probably thought I was afraid of being cut, but I was really afraid of being put to sleep. I believed that if they put me to sleep I would have no control over my life and not wake up. In reality God had all power and control.

No, in all these things we are more than conquerors
through him who loved us.
For I am convinced that neither death nor life,
neither angels nor demons,
neither the present nor the future,
nor any powers, neither height nor depth,
nor anything else in all creation,
will be able to separate us
from the love of God that is in
Christ Jesus our Lord.
Romans 8: 37-39

5

Recovery

Ooh, the pain! Oooh! What did they do to me? So much gripping pain coming from one place? I knew it would hurt, but not this bad. Oooh!

My eyes were opened, but my vision was cloudy. Everything looked to be a dismal gray. I think I had an oxygen mask on, but my mind was very groggy. I knew I had to be in the recovery room because there were other beds to the right and left of me and I could hear the moaning and groaning of the other patients. But, I could not focus on anything because of the piercing jabs in my stomach.

I saw women in white coats floating by me and figured they must be the nurses. Some were sitting at the desk in front of me. I wanted to scream out to them to help me, but they looked miles away. I could hear their voices drifting through the air as if the words were dancing to their own beat.

The only thing that seemed real around me was the gut wrenching pain I felt in my abdomen. There was no escaping it. I dared not move. I barely breathed. My stomach would contract for a few seconds, sending a wave of electrifying bolts through my entire body. I would grip the sides of the aluminum bed railing and hold on for dear life. This was worse than having a baby. I knew I had to find out what was happening to me or I would not survive this torture. I banged on the bed railings to get the nurses' attention. One came over and asked, "Are you in pain?"

No, I'm banging on the railings because I'm happy, I wanted to say. Instead I moaned, "Yessss."

"I'm going to put the morphine in your IV."

Morphine! Oh hell, I'm in trouble! The pain is going to get worse before it gets better—no wonder I'm hallucinating—God, pleassse help me! Soon enough, though, I started feeling the effects of the morphine kick in. Thank God!

As I began drifting off to sleep, members of my family started coming in to visit. I remember my cousins, Barbara Jean, Veronica, Deneen and Theresa asking me how I was doing and telling me they loved me. Theresa, who is also my God-sister, broke down crying really bad. I asked her to please not cry because I was going to be all right. Then, my mother came in with Rev, and I told them both of the tremendous agony I was experiencing. My mother went over to the nurses' station to find out what they were doing for me while my pastor stayed with me holding my hand. There were more of my family members and friends outside in the waiting room, but the nurses wouldn't allow anyone else in to see me. It didn't matter because I felt so loved and special by their overwhelming support.

Once again, I was left alone in my "dream-state" world of pain. The nurses were probably attending to the other patients or filling out charts. My stomach was having spasms on top of spasms, in spite of the morphine. Before one would finish, another had already started. It wasn't time for another dose of morphine so all I could do was grit my teeth, hold tight to the steel bars and pray that I'd get through the long night ahead.

As the night wore on, my suffering grew worse. Minute after minute, hour after hour, I must have asked the nurse twenty times for more medication. Her response was always that it wasn't time so I didn't get much sleep. I couldn't get into a comfortable position because I was too afraid to move. I didn't know if I could endure much more of this. I kept thinking that having the surgery was worse than getting shot four times! (I also wanted to know how many stitches I had because the whole front of my stomach was bandaged from top to bottom.)

Finally, late into the night, I received my dose of morphine. Again, it didn't take the pain completely away, but at least the throbbing sensations were now bearable. I was able to sleep for a few hours until my next scheduled dose. The next morning a black attendant came to wheel me to a regular room. He was the only one guiding the long bed I was lying in. My hope was that he didn't bump into anything that would cause me nothing but shear agony.

We reached room 525 without incident. There was only one bed in the room, so I knew I wouldn't have a roommate. I wondered how my 5 foot, 2 inch body and 160 pound frame was going to get from one bed to the other. I looked at the attendant who was no bigger than a minute in height and size, and knew he wouldn't be much help. As he started telling me to slide to the edge of the bed, I realized I was on my own. I struggled to move, trying not to bring on more discomfort than need be. But, ooh the pain! The attendant kept saying, "You gotta move. You can't be afraid." As I cut my eyes at him, I wanted to say, *"Shut up with your li'l self! I know I gotta move. It's my body racked with pain not yours."* But instead, I just groaned.

I made it! What a challenge, but I was still intact. The orderly left with the bed I just painstakingly inched my way out of. I was left to myself for a few minutes. A white, male nurse came into my room asking how I was doing. I looked at him with a semi-smile on my face and told him I was in pain. (What I really wanted to ask was, *"Where the hell were you when I struggled out that bed by myself?"*)

He left and came back with some codeine (They had taken me off the morphine), a wash bucket with liquid soap and a wash cloth. I washed the best I could with his assistance, not really caring what part of my body he saw. Then he placed a stiff, but clean, floral hospital gown around my body.

After the nurse left, I adjusted the bed and laid back. I tried to recall all that had occurred. None of it made any sense, no matter how many times I flipped the events over in my head. I didn't know how I was going to get through this. At that moment, I desperately needed to see my children. Tears formed in the corner of my eyes and began rolling down my round, high cheeks. I earnestly tried to unravel the tangled cobweb of thoughts from my mind and toss them into the garbage. The last thing I needed was to despair over my circumstances, sob uncontrollably, and bust my stitches.

Sometime later, doctors came in my room to examine my foot, which was broken and needed to be in a cast. Then, they pulled back the dressing to check the jillion staples that must have been in my stomach. The woman doctor who had stapled my stomach was so proud of the neat work she had done stapling around my navel and how clean the incision was. She said in her foreign accent that they had removed the bullet from my stomach and how lucky I was because the bullet did no internal damage to any of my major organs. It was just lying there, and they couldn't believe it.

"I'm not lucky, I'm blessed. See, I told y'all to leave the bullet alone. Now I have this long cut and all this pain for nothing," I amusingly replied. I was glad that the edge in my voice was gone.

She and the other doctors laughed and said they would be back later to check on me. I made sure I didn't laugh because my stomach hurt so much. I wouldn't laugh or cough for another week.

By the middle of the day the worst of the discomfort had subsided. I couldn't have felt happier because throughout the day my mother, my son Marques, Aunt Barbara Ann, Uncle Sonny, my neighbors Rob and Lavern Saunders and Luther and Sylvia Flowers came to visit me. We cried, they laughed, we talked, prayed and shook our heads. No one could believe all of what happened, especially me.

My family and friends was so relieved that I had survived it all and that I was in good spirits. They expressed their sympathy to me for Herb and concern for my children. Herb's sister Bertha and his Aunt Mary came to see how I was doing also. I told them that Herb would have tried to kill the children too, but they didn't believe me. Most of the other family members stayed away. In conversation with Bertha, I'd learned that they blamed me for what happened, which angered most of my family more than me.

I had a whole lot more to worry about than my in-laws hatred of me. So, I conserved my energy for things to come. Herby was going to die. He was on the seventh floor brain dead from a self-inflicted gunshot wound to his head at age 35. He shot me four times with a .22 caliber gun in my head, thigh, foot and buttocks—three bullets were still in me. I had to tell my children their daddy was as good as dead and plan a funeral for the man I loved and who tried to kill me. That was more than enough that I cared to deal with.

In the late afternoon of that same day, two doctors came into my room while my family was visiting to tell me that they were taking Herb off life support that night. My question to them was "Are you asking me or telling me if I want to take him off?"

They answered back that they were telling me because according to hospital policy, in certain cases they do not need the consent from the next of kin, that the hospital makes the determination.

"Well then, what is it that you want from me?"

"We would like to know if you are willing to donate any of your husband's organs? If you are, he'll stay on life support until tomorrow morning when we prep him for surgery."

The room that was once loud and noisy became very quiet and still. All these faces were looking down at me. I really felt bad for my oldest son who was sitting in the chair at the foot of my bed trying to act like none of what he just heard phased him. But I knew better. Marques had the beginnings of a mustache and sideburns that gave him the appearance of a man-child. His shoulders were drooped like they had the weight of the world on them, and his eyes had the look of a scared little boy. My baby had grown into a handsome young man during those ten months we were apart. I wondered if he blamed me, too, for the death of his dad. I watched him and thought of all that he, Corey, and Sheriah had been through, as I pondered over my decision. I choked back tears and said, "I don't know. I need to think about it. Before you take him off life support, I want to see him." The doctors looked at me as if I was crazy.

"Someone will come back later tonight to go over the options with you, and you can tell them your answer then. We'll make the arrangements for you to go upstairs tonight to see your husband."

I looked at my family after the doctors left and started crying. My Aunt Barbara Ann and Uncle Sonny told me to pray on it and not to worry. They let me know they loved me and would support my decision. I told them that Herb had an eye transplant in 1993 from a little three year old boy who had died, and how he regained seventy percent of his sight after the operation. We all knew then what my answer would be.

A young black woman attendant came to my room around 7:00 that evening with a wheelchair to take me to see Herb. My mother, Aunt Barbara Ann and my son, Marques were still at the hospital and came with me on the elevator to the seventh floor to see Herb and say goodbye.

The doctors had already informed me that his eyes would be open, but he couldn't see or respond. My mom and aunt waited outside the curtain with the aid while Marques and I saw Herb. His eyes were open, but there was no life in them.

I let Marques go to his dad first. I was sorry Corey and Sheriah could not be there, but I knew it was for the best. I heard Marq tell his dad that he loved him and that he'd miss him. I expected to see tears running down his face when he turned around, but there were none. I wanted to tell him that it was all right to cry. But, I knew he was too much like me, and had to hold onto his tough image because once the tears started, they wouldn't stop.

I rolled myself up next to Herb and looked at him from head to toe—trying to remember the man that loved me so much. His hand was so stiff and lifeless as I held it from my wheelchair. I looked into his big, pretty eyes and told him that I forgave him and was sorry things had ended this way. I looked at him one last time and turned to leave.

"Marques, are you all right? I asked.

"Yeah." He nodded.

"Are you ready to go?"

"Yeah."

Neither Marq nor I showed any emotion. I was just as numb as I had been the day before. I probably was still in a state of shock and denial. I thought seeing Herb would help release some of the emotional blockage. (Thinking back, it was probably a good thing I was numb because I don't think I would have been able to get the things done that I needed for my children and myself.)

Later that night, after my family went home, a woman doctor came to my room to go over the list of organ-donated-options and to ask for my answer. All the major and minor organs could be donated—from his heart to his eyes. She told me Herb's heart had to be beating for the doctors to remove the organs. I listened half heartedly so as to not think about the reality of Herb being dead. I told her they could have his heart, kidneys and, pancreas. I don't know why I chose those three, but I felt at peace with myself.

I also told her that that was my decision and God would have the last say so. She said okay and that the surgery would be 6:00 in the morning and someone would come to let me know when it was over. I lay there after she left, praying to God to make the final decision and to help me be strong for our children and myself.

The next morning, very early, another woman doctor came into my room holding charts in her hand and crying hysterically. She had on a dress or skirt with low black heel pump shoes. Her thin white doctor's coat was over her clothes. Her stethoscope was dangling around her neck, tucked under her shoulder length, brownish color hair. Her face was small and pale with her bangs hanging just below her forehead. I think she was the doctor in charge of overseeing Herb's donated organs.

"Mrs. Grant," she said between sobs. "I'm sorry to inform you that your husband is dead."

I looked at her in total confusion, not knowing what to say. I couldn't understand why she was crying, especially since doctors weren't suppose to show emotions like that. Of course Herb would be dead if they removed his vital organs, I thought to myself.

"It's all right Doctor. I knew my husband would die."

"No, no Mrs. Grant, you don't understand! Your husband died before we could remove any of his organs. I've never seen anything like it. His heart just stopped."

"What do you mean?"

"We prepped him for surgery and had him on the operating table and his heart stopped before we could do anything. We tried to revive him, but couldn't. I'm sorry."

"Oh my God! Thank you! You made the final decision and took it out of my hands. Thank you God! Thank you! Well, I told you God would have the last say so, and he did."

I didn't know if she was crying because Herb was dead or because she wasn't able to remove the organs first. It was really strange seeing her like that. I told her it was all right and that I was all right. She said she was sorry again and left my room with large raindrop tears still rolling down her cheeks. I envied her, though. I wished that my tears would burst forth.

My husband was now dead, really dead. The stark reality took a long time to sink in before I called my mother, pastor, and Herb's sister, Bertha, to notify them of Herb's death. My pastor was very comforting, as always. He can take the sting out of any painful experience.

I started making plans for Herb's funeral over the phone from my hospital bed. My mother and Bertha went to the mortician to finalize the arrangements. Two days after that I was released from the hospital. Having spent a total of five days there, I left with a broken foot with the bullet still in it and a bullet in my head and upper left thigh. Physically, I would heal. Emotionally, only time could heal the wounds within. (Some may never fully close.)

My husband officially died on September 10, 1996, but in my heart he died October 22, 1995, the day I left.

PART TWO

COMING FULL CIRCLE

6

Sleepless Nights

The nights were the worst time for me while I was at the University Hospital in Newark. Thoughts flooded my mind. In the stillness of the night I would lay trapped in my thoughts. Ever since I left Herby, my bed and all that was familiar to me, sleep no longer came easily. Images of my life with Herby played peek-a-boo with the visions of my life in the shelter and living in Newburgh. Life with Herby was a journey of rollercoaster rides—one minute we were up; then down; and sometimes all around.

We met each other on the track team at Ferris High School in Jersey City. When I entered as a freshman, Herby was a junior. We really didn't pay much attention to each other then, at least I didn't. I had a boyfriend named Jason I had been dating for a year, and Herb had a girlfriend. The most contact we had then was at track practice and the track meets we had almost every Saturday. The boys and girls had different coaches, but we all rode the yellow school bus together and cheered for each other as teammates of Ferris in our respective races.

I was a sprinter. I ran everything from 50 meters to a half mile. Herb ran the distant races—anything from a mile to the two mile. He was pretty good. He ran like he was sitting in a chair with his head bobbing from side to side. Above all the loud chants of "Go Herby, you can do it!" you heard Coach Smith yelling, "Grant, stop moving that head and run!" After awhile we all started singing it, "Stop moving your head and run! Stop moving your head and run!" We thought if we sang it loud and long enough, he would hold his head still. But, that became his trademark throughout the entire season and the next. He got teased for it all the time—off and on the track—and nothing ever changed.

61

Bertha Bobo, whom I grew up with in the Projects, was on the track team, too. She nicknamed me "Duck-Butt." She said when I ran my butt stuck out and I waddled like a duck down the track. Coach Walker, the freshman boys' track coach then, nicknamed me "Fingers." When I met him, the summer of my freshman year, my middle finger was broken. He was the new manager of the lifeguards at the Montgomery pool where I swam every summer before the City tore it down. He could never remember how to pronounce my name, so at the age of fourteen, he renamed me.

Due to the fact that I was a sprinter, I had to run in the trials and semi-finals in order to qualify for the finals. So, on any given Saturday during track season, which started in November and lasted well into June, I would run between four to five races a meet—not including the Mile Relay which I led off. The names, "Duck-Butt," "Quack-Quack," and "Fingers" could be heard as my teammates and coach yelled them from the bleaches or across the track, as I sprinted in the 60, 100, and 200 meter dashes, hoping to be the first one bursting through the tape. Those names have stuck with me throughout my life. Even though we weren't together then, Herby and I made quite a pair—he wagging his head and me shaking my tail.

I didn't pay much attention to Herby in those days, but by the indoor season of Herb's senior year, we became a little more interested in each other, and became more than just teammates. Personally, I think it came about because I had broken up with my boyfriend, Jason, Herb's girlfriend was moving to the South before the end of the school year, and he was in pursuit of a date for the senior prom.

Herb wasn't as attractive as some of the other boys that I knew on the track team or at school. He was short with a big nose and big eyes. But, he was very well liked, friendly, smart, a little on the quiet side and respectful toward girls. He didn't join in when the boys would tease me about being stuck-up or a virgin.

During our track meets he began coming over to where I would sit to talk to me. He would ask how many races I had to run—if I thought I would win—if I were nervous—and if he could rub my legs down with "heat." The heat was a deep orange-red color that came in a white plastic, 4 x 8 jar. It was a thick, smelly, gooey gel that was usually bitter cold because one of the coaches would leave it in the trunk of his car. We would rub our legs down with the heat about an hour before a race so it could penetrate our muscles and loosen them up.

At first, I was very self-conscious about Herb rubbing the heat on my legs, not to mention the "Woo Vonny" and accusing stares from my teammates. But, it sure felt better and different with Herby rubbing my muscles than my teammates or myself. I would strip off my green wool sweat top and pants, exposing my lean body of muscle mass and the form fitting green and gold school uniform colors which consisted of an elastic-waist cotton brief and a sleeveless tank top. I would lay flat on my stomach and on top of my sweat clothes to protect my body from the cold, dirty track with my chin resting on the criss-cross of my arms. Herb would be on both knees, bent over in his green sweats to the outside of whichever leg he was working on first. I was not able to see him because he would spread and smooth the balm out along the thickness of my thigh muscles. I would close my eyes as he began gently, but firmly, squeezing and releasing the muscle together with the tips of his fingers, starting just below my butt and stopping a little above the knee joint. Then, he would reverse the process—squeezing and releasing. Squeezing and releasing.

After he felt the muscle loosen up, he would swing one knee between the inside of my leg, leaving the other knee on the outside. I'd spread my legs slightly apart as one of his hands was on the outside and the other on the inside and his thumb tips were meeting in the middle of my thigh, pressing firmly in a circular motion up and down. I'd lay there trying to act as if I was relaxed as possible with him looking down at my body and his hands inadvertently touching the outer line of my buttocks and between my legs. I'd wonder to myself if he knew that he felt my butt and if it felt as good to him as it did to me, and what he was thinking. Once the thigh muscle was finished, he would start on my calf muscle, being sure not to squeeze too hard and then move on to the other leg.

Usually, I would give him the exact rub down later in the day. When my hand would accidentally touch his behind, a sly smile would spread across my face—knowing that I got away with something.

In March, near the end of our indoor season, we were at the 168th Street Armory in New York City. The last two times we were there, I was unable to place in the top three slots of the finals in the 60-meter dash. Coach Walker, who was now my coach because Coach Brandy had retired at the end of my freshman year, really wanted me to do better. He sent me down early to the back of the track to start warming up and to relax before my race. Herb accompanied me as he'd done pretty much for the past month. I enjoyed having him along, especially giving me my rubdowns. I didn't think his eyes and nose were so big anymore or that he was too short. In my eyes he was very handsome and easy to talk to.

Herby was really working the balm into the back of my legs with the tips of his fingers. (I think Coach said something to him.) I could feel the penetration of the heat in my thigh muscle by the time he massaged my calf—and the same with the other leg. I flipped over so he could perform the ritual on the front of my muscles. I sat up and leaned back on my hands for support with my eyes closed as Herb's fingers moved up and down and in between the sides of my legs. When I opened my eyes to look at him, he asked me if I would go to his prom. I couldn't believe it. I don't remember much after that moment or how I did in the race, but it didn't matter because I was going to the prom just like I'd predicted some months earlier.

At the end of each school year, the prom committee would post the date for the next year's prom. I was running down the red, cement stairwell in school with my best friend, Sharon, at the end of our freshman year, and there in front of us on an 8" x 10" yellow piece of construction paper that was hanging on the brick wall, was the sign that read:

THE
1978 SENIOR CLASS PROM
JUNE 1, 1978
AT THE MANOR
IN
WEST ORANGE, NJ

I screamed for Sharon to look as I jumped up and down pointing to the sign.

"Look at what?" She said.

"The sign for the senior prom. It's on my birthday!"

"Oh yeah! It sure is!"

"I'm going to that prom!"

"How you going to the prom? You don't even know anybody!"

"So what! I'm going. I'll go with anybody—don't care—as long as I get there. It's on my birthday."

I sang the rest of the way down the stairs, "I'm going to the prom, I'm going to the prom." We laughed even harder with a sparkling gleam of light in our eyes as we headed out the front doors of the school to start our summer vacation.

That's what flashed through my mind, sitting on the track getting my rub down when I heard Herb ask the magic question.

Unfortunately, the prom wasn't half as exciting for me as it was preparing for it. First, were introductions. Herb and my mother had to meet each other, and she had to say "yes" to me going to the prom with him. After she gave her approval and said he seemed to be a respectable young man, I wasted no time searching for a pattern, material, shoes, pocketbook, and jewelry. Sharon was my accomplice in the entire matter—going in and out of stores with me and giving her humble opinion on each item I chose.

My biggest dilemma was make-up and my hair. I didn't wear make-up or know how to apply it. Frankly, I thought it made me look fake and really didn't care for it—and I had worn my hair in an Afro since the fifth grade and wanted a different style for the prom. I figured I'd ask my older cousins, Vanessa and Barbara Jean, about all that later. In the meantime, I needed to meet Herb's mother so that she could take my measurements and begin making my gown. Herb told me when he first asked me to go to the prom that his mother was a seamstress and had offered to make my gown.

They lived in the downtown part of Jersey City on Bowman Street. I walked the twenty-minute walk from the Projects by myself wishing that Herby were going to be home.

Mrs. Grant was a small-framed, dark skinned woman, who still spoke with a touch of her southern accent. The skin around her face was very puffy, especially under her eyes. I could tell she was older than my mother because she had a lot of strands of gray hair and the fact that her oldest daughter was thirty-years-old. We were alone in her bedroom when she took my body measurements, but I was so scared she wouldn't like me that my teeth chattered.

Her bedroom was much bigger than my mother's and my bedroom which could easily have fit into hers with space left over. There was a mantle with a fake fireplace, a black leather recliner that had seen better days, a full-sized bed with an old frayed chest on the hardwood floor at the foot of the bed, and the highest ceilings I had ever seen. The rest of the space was composed of all her sewing gadgets.

The Singer sewing machine looked like a wooden table until she lifted the top and up popped the white machine all intact. There were swatches of all kinds of colored material that she said she made quilts out of—a brown wicker basket with packs of different sized needles, and spools of green, blue, and black thread.

While taking my measurements she remarked on how skinny I was and how big my behind was for someone my size. I was 5'2" tall—115 pounds, with a 32B breast size and a 24 inch waist, which made my behind that much more noticeable. I smiled at her comment because I'd heard it all my life from my own mother and family members, "Vonny got a big ole butt," and knew from her smile, that she liked me.

The day of the prom finally arrived and so did my sixteenth birthday. I didn't go to school that day. Instead, I took my cousins' advice and made an appointment for early that morning to get my hair permed. I also had to go to the florist after that to pick up the carnation I was giving to Herb to wear on the lapel of his suit. I asked the florist to spray it a light navy blue. I took a nap after I returned home—careful not to mess up my curly permed Afro.

My mother woke me up around 4:30 in the afternoon. I ran my bath water, making sure it was cool enough so that my curls wouldn't drop. I washed and used a lot more soap than usual under my arms because I was going to shave for the first time. My gown was sleeveless, and this was the first formal affair that I was going to. I bought the white and red can of Neat that I always saw the white girls in the locker room at school use (They were *always* shaving something!)

I dried off and followed the directions on the can, making sure that I shook it well, and held it approximately six inches away. The white spray foamed up under my left arm as I waited for the directed time to start removing the hair. Within a minute after spraying the Neat, I came bolting out of the bathroom butt naked, screaming for my mother. She came running down the hallway yelling, "What's the matter? What's the matter?"

"It's burning! It's burning!" I yelled, frantically.

"What's burning?" my mother yelled back as she was ushering me back into the bathroom.

"My underarm, Mommy! It's burning! Ooh, it burns."

She immediately threw a wash cloth in the sink, running cold water on it and placed it under my burning arm. It offered relief temporarily, but my skin was so red by this time that the cold cloth didn't help much. My mother asked what happened after she saw I had calmed down.

"I sprayed that stupid Neat under my arm to remove the hair like I'd seen the white girls at school do. It ain't never burn them."

My mother looked at me, shook her head and began to laugh. I started laughing in between sobs, too, because not a bit of hair came off from under my arm—it was for shaving legs.

She got some baby powder and sprinkled it under my arm. That helped sooth the irritation. With my mother's help I continued to get ready for the big night. I got on my underclothes, coffee colored stockings and my 2 1/2 inch high heel, sling back blue shoes. I also wrapped myself in a towel to allow my underarm to air out a little longer before putting on my beautiful light gray gown.

My gown was made with taffeta, silk material. It had a square or boxed shaped neckline with a scallop shaped cape attached to it. The cape hung midway to my back, draping over my shoulders, down to my elbows. The bodice of the gown flared out slightly from my waist, touching the top of my foot.

By the time Herb arrived in his father's 1977 sky blue Pontiac Catalina, I was fully dressed. My cousin Barbara Jean loaned me her blue and gray silk-fringed shawl to wear over my gown. That helped me to hide my hairy underarms and the red pimpled bumps that had formed. It also matched the colors we were wearing, enhancing my gown. I decided to wear a dab of blue eye shadow, wine colored lipstick and a navy blue, flower comb in the side of my hair like Billie Holiday.

Herb looked very handsome in the gray, pin-stripped suit his mother made, white shirt, blue tie, and shiny blue shoes. I pinned the carnation onto his label without sticking myself when he came into the house, and he gave me a beautiful light blue, wrist carnation corsage. I was all smiles, forgetting about my deformed underarm when we drove off.

The festive atmosphere was electric. The green lawn was immaculate under the bright colorful lights that lit up the sky, setting the tone for a magnificent evening. The beautiful array of flowers that etched out the walkway and entrance to the towering sculpture of a building scented the cool spring night's air. We poured out of our cars to the awaiting festivities.

The young ladies' and men's faces were aglow as Herb and I stepped into the room where the hors d'oeuvre were being served. There was a sea of black/white, blue/gray, brown/beige, gray/burgundy, and red/white gowns and tuxedos—with each couple wearing matching color schemes. My eyes couldn't take in the beautiful sights fast enough to get an outline of each unique gown. But, my eyes did catch the huge fish tanks of broiled shrimp and cocktail sauce. I nudged Herb to walk in that direction as we said our "Hello's," "What UP's," and "Ya'll look great!"

I'd never tasted anything so delicious. The hot tanginess of the cocktail sauce kept me reaching for more, but it was soon time to start moving into the ballroom where the main course was being served. Herb laughed at my poked out lips and reluctance to leave. He persuaded me by telling me that the other food would be just as good.

We sat at a beautiful candlelit decorated table with four other couples who were seniors. One of Herb's closest friends didn't like the fact that Herb brought an underclassman to the prom and wouldn't include me in the conversations. I didn't care and interjected my opinions anyway.

The waiters and waitresses brought out our food covered with a silver tin lid. When the waiter sat mine in front of me and lifted off the lid, my eyes almost popped out of my head. The string beans or green beans (as they were called) looked like waxed flowers and tasted even worse; my potato was decorated in the shape of a mountain with brown ridges going around it; and the steak or prime rib was as red as the bumps under my arm. Herb caught my expression and started laughing uncontrollably. When he regained his composure, I leaned over to his ear and said, "Just as good, huh." That set off another round of laughter.

When dinner was officially over, we got up to dance. As I passed the tables to get to the dance floor, I could tell everybody had a similar reaction as mine from all the food that was left on the plates. Herb and I tried to dance to the rhythm of "Brick House" that was being drummed out by the live band of white musicians. We got so tired of getting out of beat, off step and laughing from their out-of-tune singing that we left the dance floor and decided to go for a walk. We walked through the moon lit night to an isolated spot in the beautiful, colorful garden under some trees, holding hands.

"So Herb," I said, "This is what a prom is, huh?"

"Yeah, I know it's pretty boring."

"It wouldn't be so boring if the music was good. Why didn't

they just hire a DJ instead of a white band that can't play soul music?"

"I don't know, but you sure look good."

Before I could respond, his mouth was on mine, parting my lips with his warm, moist tongue and his big hands were around my waist pulling me closer to him. My body was shining just as brightly on the inside as the full moon. We stayed liked that for a long time.

A few days after the prom my old boyfriend, Jason and I got back together. I knew I had hurt Herb's feelings and told him that I was sorry. He never showed that he was angry; he just said, "When you and Jason break up, I'll be right there to move in." I smiled and knew we would be good friends for a long time.

I was glad that Jason and I had an open relationship where we could date other people. So I continued to maintain a close, friendly relationship with Herb for two years while he attended Glassboro State College in South Jersey. We kept in touch with each other through letters and telephone calls, and he would come to visit me either at my home or high school when he was out on a break.

Towards the end of my senior year, I broke up with Jason for the hundredth time. That was finally it. A few days later, Herb expressed an interest in attending my graduation and taking me out dancing so I gave him the ticket to the ceremony. We went to Club 88 in New York City that night with another couple and danced the evening away. After that wonderful day and night in June of 1980, we would become inseparable.

Herby and I dated the entire summer. We went to the movies—the park—Atlantic City—his house—my house—anywhere we could be together, we went. The most fun for me was when he came to my grandfather's house, where I was living after my grandmother died. We would sit on the green couch in the living room and watch the football game and snuggle up close to each other and cheer on the teams in between our touching and tongue kissing sessions. He didn't express any sexual frustration, which won my heart. He was just surprised to find out how much I loved football, but pleased.

70

Herb was strictly a Dallas Cowboy's fan. The Dallas Cowboys, Pittsburgh Steelers, Minnesota Vikings and the Los Angles Rams were my favorite teams. I loved Roger Starbauch and Drew Pearson from the Cowboys—Len Swan and Franco Harris from the Steelers—Fran Tarkington and somebody else from the Vikings—and Eric Dickinson from the Rams. They were all great and good-looking. But I felt so sorry for the Minnesota Vikings because they lost all four times they went to the Super Bowl.

So many thoughts and memories of Herb and our life together as two young people learning to love would go though my mind during those sleepless nights. I'd lie there, asking myself again and again, *"Where and when did it all go wrong—from the hallways and track team of Ferris High School to the bedroom at 64 Canter Street, some sixteen years later?"*

Trust in the Lord with all your heart
and lean not on your own
understanding;
in all your ways acknowledge him,
and he will make your paths straight.
Proverbs 3:5-6

7

REV

I could hear the tic-tock of the gold clock sitting on the nightstand ticking in the calm of the night. The hospital was so deadly quiet that it seemed later than 11:00 p.m. I knew this would be another sleepless night and that I would be awake for a few more hours so I turned the television on again, making sure the sound was down low. I'd hoped by watching TV I would drift off to sleep. Instead, my thoughts wandered back to 1995 when our marriage had deteriorated to a shell and I had begun to take Herb's threats of killing me more seriously.

I started attending a Clinical Pastoral Education workshop in March and began learning about loving myself and healing the wounds of my past. This was seven months prior to my leaving Herb. The sessions were being offered at Neptune Baptist Church in Jersey City where I had attended for a short while. The pastor of the church recommended that I attend the class after I confided to him about the "calling" that I believed I'd received from God in December of 1994. He explained that the course would help me understand more about who I was, my life in the past and present, the purpose and plan God had for my life and how it was related to my "calling."

There were about thirteen or fourteen of us in the church hall that served as our classroom. It was a large open space room with a stage, kitchen and bathroom. The lessons would be taken from the Bible, and we would analyze the scriptures in the way they applied to our lives. That was a different process for me, but interesting. It was almost therapeutic.

Reverend J. Edward Lewis was the professor for the class. He was from Newburgh, New York and a therapist at a treatment facility for addicts and alcoholics. He was also an adjunct professor at New York Theology Seminary. Reverend Lewis was over six feet tall and had a receding hairline. He was dark skinned with thick, black-rimmed glasses that made his eyes look like he was always squinting. He also had a full goatee that gave him a look of wisdom. His style of clothing, which mainly consisted of corduroy pants, plaid shirts or sweaters, was plain and somewhat outdated.

The first evening after class I approached him to ask a question about submission. Herb and I were arguing a lot about my "calling" and the amount of time I was spending studying the Bible to understand my life. He would throw the scripture from Ephesians 5:23 up in my face about the husband being the head of the wife and how I was supposed to submit to him by doing what he said. I was so tired of hearing that and telling him he must first submit to Christ before I submitted to him. I needed a quick-fix answer fast, and I hoped Reverend Lewis would give it to me.

"Hi Reverend Lewis, my name is Lavon Grant and there's a question I've been wondering about. I hope you can answer it."

"Hello Mrs. Grant, it's nice to meet you. What is your question?"

"Is a woman supposed to be submissive to her husband in everything, even when she knows he's wrong?"

He stood there looking at me with a canny smile on his face and said, "I can't answer that."

"What do you mean you can't answer that?" I snapped back.

He maintained his composure and continued speaking in his soft, well-mannered voice saying, "Well, I would need to know more of the circumstances, and we don't have enough time right now."

"But you're a reverend, right?"

"Yes."

"So as a reverend, you should have the answer to the question. Other reverends give an answer."

"Okay. But I can't give you an answer right now until I know more."

I glared at him with fire in my eyes, not knowing what else to say to make him change his mind. I was desperate for an answer though. We stood there a moment looking at each other. I was so disgusted with him that I turned to leave. All I could think about when I marched off with my tail swinging from side to side in my black dress was how I was never going back—that stupid smile on his face and how bad I wanted to slap it off—I bet then he would've had some answers.

But, I returned Friday after Friday, determined that he was going to give me an answer. Each time I asked the question, he responded the same, leaving me more frustrated than before. Eventually, I stopped asking but continued to respond to his questions sarcastically and letting him know I had no problems.

One day I got to class early. No one was there yet so I sat in the church hall at the table reading Psalms 119. When I looked up, I saw Reverend Lewis walking into the hall. He was carrying his brown cloth bag and chart stand. It was too late for me to get up and leave because he had already seen me. I sat there looking down at my Bible, hoping that he wouldn't come and sit next to me. But, he did.

"Hi Mrs. Grant. How are you this fine evening?" He said all chippery.

"Hi Reverend Lewis," I said as dry as I could, hoping that he would go away.

"What are you reading?"

"The Bible!" I snorted, rolling my eyes.

"I know that, but which book?"

"Psalms."

"Okay, good book. Do you go to Neptune?"

"No, not anymore. I returned to Missionary Baptist a month ago, where my husband goes."

"How long have ya'll been going there?"

"Well, my husband's family been going a long time, but I started going when we got married nine years ago. I was a Catholic before then."

"I see," he said shaking his head. Then he asked, "Is your family still Catholic or Baptist?"

"Well, uh, don't know. We all started out Catholic and went to Catholic school. Then my mother became a Muslim when she married a so-called Muslim and we had to start going to the Mosque." I could see that cunning smile starting to form at the corners of his mouth, but I continued. "We had to stop eating pork, celebrating Christmas, birthdays and everything else. Woo, I hated that! Excuse me! Anyway, I think some of my sisters, brothers and cousins are still Catholic, but they don't go to Mass. I think my mother is still a Muslim, but she doesn't practice it—at least she doesn't go to the Mosque—I don't know what she is. One of my sisters is a Muslim now. My Aunt Eleanor is a Catholic, and my Aunt Barbara Ann and Uncle Sonny are Baptist—they go to this church."

"And are you a Baptist?"

"Yup, I am. I just don't like all the traditions that Baptist hold onto."

"Like what?"

"Oh, like you can't wear pants to church, or that women don't belong in the pulpit, or how everyone always says, 'This is the way we always did it,' or being submissive to your husband. You know, things like that."

He smiled and asked where was my father. None of your business is what I wanted to say, but I said, "He lives in Boston. No, I mean Massachusetts—yeah, somewhere in Massachusetts. I don't know where. I haven't seen him in a long time."

"Why did he leave?"

Gosh, he asks a lot of questions. "Because he was on drugs, and my mother divorced him, only to marry another drug addict."

"Which drug?"

"Huh. Oh, heroin, both of them. That's what everybody used in the 70's."

"What is he doing now?"

"I don't know! But he's not on drugs anymore. He drinks. I think he's an alcoholic."

"And your husband—does he drink?"

"No. He's been a recovering alcoholic for two years now."

"Do you know it's not a coincidence that you married your husband, and he's an alcoholic?"

"No. What are you talking about?" I asked with caution and raised eyebrows.

"Was your father's father an alcoholic? And Herb's father?"

"Yeah and yeah."

Just when he had my interest, other people from the class started coming in, and he said we would finish talking later. I couldn't help myself, but I begged him to please tell me what he meant when he said it was no accident that I married Herb and he was an alcoholic. But he only smiled.

After the rest of the class got there, we read from the Book of Luke, Chapter 17, Verses 20-37. I allowed myself to open up to his teachings to hear what other things he might say about my life that I didn't know. I had read that part of scripture several times before, but for whatever reason Verses 20, 21 and 37 stuck out for me.

Reverend Lewis began to read, 20: "Once, having been asked by the Pharisees when the kingdom of God would come, Jesus replied, 'The kingdom of God does not come with your careful observation;' 21: nor will people say, 'Here it is,' or 'There it is,' because the kingdom of God is within you."

Rev continued reading, but I didn't hear him anymore. Light bulbs were turning on in my head. If the kingdom of God is within me, I thought, why have I been searching outside of myself all this time for who I was and my purpose in life? *Oh my God! The answers have been within me all this time. Why didn't anyone ever tell me that? And why am I just hearing the meaning of that scripture now when I've read it before?* Oh, I had so many questions to ask Reverend Lewis. By the time I heard him again, he was on the last verse of 37: "Where, Lord?" they asked. He replied, "Where there is a dead body, there the vultures will gather."

What a profound scripture, I thought, but Reverend Lewis' questions were even more profound. He asked the class, "What is dead in your life, and who are the vultures?"

Silence. No one moved. I stopped breathing, hoping to become invisible or a part of the table. I could tell from the way that the other thirteen students kept their heads down so did they. From that day on, my attitude toward Rev began to change, and I began to understand that I was responsible for my own happiness—not Herb, my children or other people, as I had thought. Eventually, I stopped blaming Herb for why I was miserable and understood that everything in life happened for a reason and there were lessons I needed to learn through my experiences in order to grow, whether they were good or bad. Most importantly, I began to understand far too well the problems I had and how serious they were.

I stressed upon Herby how significant the process of going within himself to find answers in order to grow was as an individual and to our marriage, but to no avail. He didn't want to hear what I had to say. He just wanted me to stop going to the classes. I kept going to the class, and Reverend Lewis continued to silence us with his profound questions. His mannerism reminded me of the food brands in the no-frills aisles at the supermarket, for once you open the can or unwrap the package and the contents, they are just as good or better than the name brand.

One day as we were getting close to the sessions being over, Rev read from the Book of John, Chapter 5, Verses 1-9. It was about the man who was an invalid and stayed by the pool for thirty-eight years in the same condition, and Jesus asking him if he wanted to get well. When Reverend Lewis finished reading, he commented on the man being at the pool for thirty-eight years, making little movement or none at all in his life. I thought to myself as I sat there how I didn't want to be stuck in the same place for that length of time and have nothing to show for it. Then, reality hit me that I was already thirty-three years old and didn't know where my life was going. I wondered if the others were thinking what I was thinking.

Reverend Lewis interrupted my thoughts and asked the class, "Do you want to get well? And, if you do, at what cost?"

For me, that last question really was the qualifier to the first question. I thought a moment at what cost did I want to get well. I was already pretty miserable so I told myself what difference did it make at what cost it took to get well—anything had to be better than where I already was. I was scared to death to speak, but I raised my hand anyway.

"Yes Mrs. Grant. Lavon. Vonny," Rev said.

I smiled and said, "I want to get well."

Rev was sitting across the table from me and looked directly into my eyes and asked, "At what cost?"

For the first time, I didn't turn away from his intense stare and said in a determined voice, "At whatever cost it takes!"

"You're sure?" Rev asked.

"I'm positive!" I knew there was no backing down now.

After that time in 1995, I began to apply to career positions that were related to my field of study in Marketing. I had been working for two years as a substitute teacher in the Jersey City School system, and was too afraid to have a more challenging job due to Herb's lack of support at home and with the children, our zillion problems, and mainly, my own fears and self-doubt. I no longer worked or planned around Herb's controlling behavior. If there was something I didn't feel comfortable doing or wanted to do, I just told him no.

I remember while working as a substitute teacher, Herb demanded I call him at work if the school didn't need me for the day, he would tell me what things he needed for me to do. I laughed as usual and told him he must be crazy if he thought I was going to report to him and find out how I needed to spend my days off. He was furious. He started yelling at me, saying that I never listen, I never let him be the man and how selfish I was. I was shocked at his degree of anger because I didn't realize he was really serious. I wouldn't change my position and never called him, which caused many more arguments later.

My self-esteem and confidence were growing. I no longer had the energy nor the time to argue with Herby about money; his gambling habit; my lack of cooking and cleaning; what my role was as a wife and mother; the church; my clothes; God; when I should or should not go out or with whom; and all the other millions of trivial things we couldn't agree on, like the color of the sky. I would just walk away in the midst of an argument, leaving him yelling at me about how many types of bitches I was.

By September, I was no longer the Lavon who would always fix the problems (believing that's what I was suppose to do even if I didn't create them), or would take care of everybody else—or the Lavon who believed that her identity came from being married to Herb or being a mother. The new Lavon had begun to learn to love herself the way she wanted others (namely Herb) to love her unconditionally.

Also, during that time Herby would tell me a different story almost everyday of how he wanted to kill me and why. One day we were at Red Lobster eating dinner. Surprisingly, we were having a pretty good time. Out of the blue, Herby said in between laughs, very nonchalantly, if he had money he would hire a hit man to kill me. I laughed too because I thought he was joking again. He continued to laugh, but said he wasn't joking. I asked him why he wanted me dead. He simply replied because he didn't know what else to do with me. Just as I blocked out his threats in the past and didn't know how to respond or act; I did the same thing at that moment and continued eating my shrimp platter.

Another time while watching television in our bedroom, Herby blurted out, "Babe, at work all I think about are ways to kill you."

Herby was lying next to me at the foot of the bed. I said, "What?" turning my head to look at him. He had a straight face— nothing visibly appeared wrong with him—there weren't two heads growing out of his neck, and he wasn't foaming at the mouth. His features were those of my husband and his voice sounded like his own. He repeated the exact words about killing me again while I was looking at him. "Babe, at work all I think about are ways to kill you." There was no mistake. I did not hear him wrong the first time.

Since his threats of killing me had become a frequent routine in our life, I'd decided to humor him. I dragged out the "*Why*

Herby? Why would you want to kill poor lil' ole me?" I was looking down at him with my arms folded across my chest and my eyes rolled back in my head, and he was looking up at me and said, "Because you have changed and I know you're gonna leave me and I can't handle that."

His words did not scare me. I merely reached out and touched his shoulder, assuring him that I wasn't going anywhere, but he shook his head and explained further. He said, "Lavon, change is good. I'm glad you're doing more and more things for yourself. I know I need to change, too, but I can't. So because I can't change and you have, I have to kill you before you leave me."

I actually burst out laughing—not able to hold it in any longer and told him that was the craziest thing I had ever heard him say and that his logic made absolutely no sense. But, he still had a serious look on his face so I indulged him some more and asked him how would he kill me. He told me he would shoot me in the head.

"Gosh Herb, that's gonna hurt," I said. "Would you shoot me while I'm sleeping or awake?"

He said it didn't matter, and he would kill the kids, too. That caused me to blink my eyes real fast and shake my head. I asked him in a semi-serious tone why he would kill the kids when they haven't done anything to him. He didn't answer me right away. Instead, he said he would kill himself, as well.

I look back now and know I should have been high-tailing my butt out of there as fast as I could, but I rationalized in my head that there was no way Herby would do this because life was supposed to be different for us. We were both college-educated, he knew right from wrong, he loved us, he didn't look crazy and I really didn't believe him and was even more curious to hear his answers as to why he felt the need to kill all of us.

Herby fulfilled my curiosity as he went into detail explaining everything. He said, "Lavon, we are good parents, and I know I'd go to jail for killing you. I can't take the chance that our families will take care of our children like us so I'd have to kill them.

Because I can't be locked up like an animal I would have to kill myself, too, but I would definitely kill you first."

"Herby, would you really kill me? I asked again.

"Yeah, Lavon. I told you, I'll shoot you in the head."

All I could say was, "Wow Herb, you really need some help."

The last time Herby threatened to kill me was over the phone. It was toward the end of October, and I had joined a swimming class at night. The class met once a week for an hour and a half and was about a twenty minute ride from where we lived. I had cooked and fed Corey and Sheriah. I was just waiting for Marques to arrive home from school so that he could watch them while I was gone.

Herb had called from work during that time to say hello and to make sure we were all right. He worked the 6:00 p.m. to 2:30 a.m. shift at the Post Office. I told him everybody was fine and reminded him that that was the night I went swimming. In a demanding tone of voice, he said he didn't want me to go. I asked him why, and he said because he didn't want me to leave the kids alone. I assured him the kids would be all right with Marques for such a short period of time. He screamed through the phone that I better not go and slammed the phone down in my ear.

Marques finally came home from school around 6:30 p.m. I asked him how was school and fixed him a plate of food. I shrugged off Herb's angry outburst and gave Marques the same instructions I had given him every week—call Ms. Sylvia's house if something's wrong, don't open the door for anyone and stay in the same room as Corey and Sheriah.

Marques was thirteen and a sensible young man. I trusted him and was out the door for my class. When I came back around 8:30 p.m., my children were in the basement watching television. Marques told me his dad had called and wanted me to call him. I went upstairs to take a shower, deciding I would call Herby later.

After I came out of the shower and put on a clean nightgown, I went downstairs to start braiding Sheriah's hair. That was when Herb called again. He wanted to know why I had gone swimming when he instructed me not to. I told him to leave me alone, reminding him how there had been no problem two nights ago when he took me out to eat at Red Lobster and left Marques at home with the younger children for two hours. He was livid that I presented that to him so lightheartedly. He yelled at me in a horrifying voice saying, "BITCH, you better be out my house by the time I get home, or I'm gonna kill your stupid ass and you better not take my children, you stupid ass bitch." Then he slammed the phone down in my ear.

I tried to dismiss Herb's extreme drama as I usually did, but his behavior had become very erratic and unpredictable over the last several months. One minute he loved me very much; the next minute, he wanted a divorce—me out of *his* house, and in the midst of it all, he would threaten to kill me. Then, he would tell me he didn't mean it; how sorry he was; how much he loved me and couldn't live without me; and then, he would beg me to stay and send me flowers the next day.

I resumed braiding Sheriah's hair, but the nagging feeling had begun tugging at the pit of my stomach. I thought back to the hundreds of threats Herb had told me in the form of stories. The vision of him coming home at 3:00 in the morning, shooting me in the head while I was asleep and unable to defend myself, caused me to jump up off the floor and yell for my children to pack a bag.

It was 11:00 p.m. by the time Marques, Corey, Sheriah, and I were loaded up in the black Jeep. I was headed for the Garden State Parkway that would lead me to Route 17 in Paramus and then onto the New York State Thruway. My children had no clue where we were going. Neither did I once we got off the Thruway. They sat very quietly and still as we rode through the night. It was as if they knew that the security of their world was about to tumble down. So did I.

I had learned my way to Newburgh when Herb and I were going to marriage counseling with Reverend Lewis in the early part of September. We would drive up, leaving Marques home with Corey and Sheirah and instructions to call Herb's sister Bertha in the event of an emergency. She only lived five minutes away. Herb had decided out of the blue that we were going to go for counseling. We had discussed it awhile back, but Herb wouldn't agree to it. One day, he came home from work and announced that he had spoken to Reverend Lewis about counseling us and that everything was set. I said, "Okay."

We met Reverend Lewis at the church where he was Assistant Pastor. It was in the City of Newburgh. He had given Herb the directions over the phone. We had gone to two counseling sessions when Herb said it wasn't working fast enough, and he decided we would stop going.

I wasn't sure if I would remember my way back to Newburgh in the dark, but I found my way and stopped at a Hess gas station in town to ask for directions to the nearest motel. The gas attendant on duty gave me the directions to Route 32 in New Windsor and said I would see several motels on the right side of the road. I was a bundle of nerves as I drove through the dark streets of a town that I was going to spend the night in and, where I knew only one person.

I found the small motel and checked in with my children. I had to use my American Express card because I had no money. I dared not look into my children's faces as we stood at the ivory desk waiting for the approval of the card to go through. I feared that the card would be denied, and we would have no other choice but to go back home. The card was accepted, and I had no idea how I was going to pay the bill once it arrived.

We walked down the dimly lit hall to our room. It had two full size beds with matching floral green comforters and curtains. The beige carpet on the floor was thin, but clean. The 19-inch, remote control color TV sat on top of the long wooden dresser. That was the first thing the kids turned on after putting their bags down anywhere. Although it was late, the sound from the television was a reprieve from the static in my head. I lay down on the bed not exactly sure when my children or I fell asleep.

When I woke up in the early hours of the morning, the television was still on, and my children were fast asleep on top of the comforter with their clothes on. I did not want to wake them so I took the comforter from my bed and placed it over them. I turned the TV off and returned back to bed. I slid under the top white sheet for cover and waited for the first break of daylight to call Reverend Lewis.

I reached Reverend Lewis at his office because I had dozed too long to call him at home. I explained what had happened and where we were. He already knew Herby and I were having major difficulties, but I never mentioned to him about the death threats until then. He asked me why, and the only answer I had for him at the time was that I really didn't believe Herb would try to kill the kids or me. He asked if I would go into a shelter because of the serious danger that I was in. I told him no, but that I would figure out something and thanked him for his love and support. He made me promise him that I would be careful and safe before we hung up.

In spite of Reverend Lewis' concerns, I made the decision to return home. I had no money, no place to go, or a plan of what I was doing and three scared children. I was still in denial that Herb's threats of killing me were real.

For the first time in my adult life, I didn't have even a vague notion of what to do. I was trapped by a wave of emotions that constantly thrashed against the base of my skull. Home was no longer the secure refuge it had once been for my children and me. I felt like I was surrounded by the Red Sea, except it wasn't Pharaoh's army I was trying to escape from. It was my own husband.

NOW faith is the substance
of things hoped for,
the evidence of things not seen.
Hebrews 11:1

8

Choices and Consequences

When I returned home, there was something distinctly different in the atmosphere. Although Herb worked the night shift at the Post Office and all day at Carol Communication, there was still tension in the air that I could cut with a knife. I knew in my heart and spirit that it was no longer safe for me to be there. The same day I arrived, I began planning to leave.

Later in the day I drove to Jersey City with my children to talk to my mother. I told her what had been going on in my marriage, especially for the last seven months. I had also mentioned to her the suggestion Rev made about me going into a shelter for awhile. She was shocked and surprised to hear about all the death threats Herb had made and even more so that I never said anything. She agreed with Reverend Lewis' advice about me going into the shelter, even after I made it known to her that if I went into a shelter, I would not stay in New Jersey; I would go to upstate New York. I was too ashamed and embarrassed for anyone I knew to find out that my marriage was failing and that I was going to be living in a Battered Women's Shelter.

In addition, we discussed what to do about Marques. I'd told my mother that it was best for him to remain with Herb until we could work things out because he was thirteen, in high school, and that the shelter might not take him. My mother and I also agreed that my children were in no danger as long as I was not around. She stated that she would support whatever decisions I made and then advised me not to go back home until Herb had gotten some help. I lay down on her bed and cried because of the distressing choices that were in front of me.

Two days later, I left Herb again. I took as many clothes as possible. I threw them in the back of the Jeep still on the hangers while Herb was at work. I packed Corey's and Sheriah's clothes into two suitcases, along with the .38 caliber gun Herb had in the house for the last nine years. I explained to Marques the night before that Corey, Sheriah, and I would be gone when he woke up in the morning. I didn't have to go into much detail because Marques had heard all the screaming and arguing between us. I did let him know that I was leaving him with his dad because we would be living in a shelter for awhile and that I thought he was too old. I told him if he'd rather come with me he could. He shook his head no and lowered his eyes. I touched his cheek softly, letting him know that it was all right. I assured him that I loved him very much and would come back home as soon as I thought it was safe. I also apologized to him for not being able to keep us all together. He said he understood, but I think he only said it believing that's what I wanted to hear. My son's face was so sad and it looked as if he had aged ten years.

The next morning I was en route to upstate New York to stay in the same motel we had been at a few days before. Once we got off the Thruway at Exit 17, I stopped at a McDonald's to get Corey and Sheriah something to eat. I drove through the drive-in-window and ordered them a #2 combination with hash browns, eggs, biscuits, bacon and a small orange juice. (I was practically penniless, but my mother had given me some money.) I parked the Jeep by the grass in the lot so my children could settle down to eat.

While they were eating, I decided to call Herby from the phone booth in front of me to let him know that I was gone. I had left him sleeping when I packed up the kids that morning. I also wanted to find out how Marques was doing. The phone call was more difficult than I expected. I never anticipated Herby pleading with me and becoming so distraught over my leaving. I thought he would have been relieved that I was gone and agreed with me that a separation was the best thing for us. My head began to hurt, and suddenly I was crying. I prayed that I wouldn't fall apart in a McDonald's parking lot where no one knew my two children or me. I walked back to the Jeep wiping my eyes. I opened the door and slid in the driver's side holding my head down. Corey and Sheriah had finished eating and continued to entertain themselves with some of their favorite toys that I had brought along. They never looked up to see my tear-stained face as I watched them out of the rear view mirror. I lay my head against the headrest and closed my eyes. The feeling of being so detached and becoming unglued while driving up the Garden State Parkway and Thruway came flooding back. I needed a bed in a hurry to support the weight of grief that I had been carrying on my shoulders. I started up the Jeep and drove out of the parking lot to find the motel. Corey and Sheriah didn't have a care in the world because they thought we were out on a breakfast adventure trip.

We arrived at the Lodge Motel and checked in. There was a fat white man at the front desk, instead of the skinny white woman who had been there before. I paid for one night with my American Express card as I'd done previously. The stocky man handed me the slip to sign and the keys to the room. I signed my name as fast as I could and began searching for Room 218. It had only been four hours since I left home, but I felt like I'd gone through a time capsule and crossed over into somebody else's life.

The room was a replica of the other one, except it was further down the long, narrow carpeted hallway and water dripped from the faucet leaving a brown, rust stain in the sink. I lay across the bed holding my throbbing head, trying to convince myself for the thousandth time that I made the right decision. The conversation I had with Herb played itself over and over in my mind like a broken record. Herb's pleas for me to come back had genuinely shaken me. The problem was I actually wanted to go back, but I knew Herb's threats of killing me would increase—and might come true.

(Go back to what?) Spun from one side of my head to the other. *(We don't make each other happy anymore)* swirled in the other direction. *(Herby doesn't want to change)* completed the tic-tac-toe that formed in my head. I thought my brain was going to turn into silly-putty from the overload of questions. Thank God my children knew how to

keep themselves busy while watching TV because I was in no shape to give them any attention.

That evening we went out to eat dinner at Burger King. After eating, Corey and Sheriah played in the indoor gym. I watched them jumping up and down in the balls having fun. I hoped they would exert as much energy as possible so they would go fast to sleep when we returned to the motel. The night was quiet and uneventful back in the room. We all eventually drifted off to sleep with the television watching us.

We checked out of the motel at 10:00 the next morning. I had driven north on Route 32, following the directions Reverend Lewis had given me to the domestic violence agency in Newburgh. First, I met him at a bagel shop on the way. He gave me last words of encouragement, telling me to keep my head up. I believe he knew that what little confidence I had the day before was now gone.

My children and I walked up the cement steps of the YMCA building on Grand Street, hand and hand. They still didn't know why we were in a strange town. We entered through the heavy glass door and walked up another flight of stairs. When we reached the top of the stairs, the agency was to our left. I took a deep breath and stepped into the office holding a little tighter to my children's hands.

We were met with a friendly smile and a "Can I help you?" from a white, thin woman behind the desk. My eyes darted nervously around the drab office. Beads of sweat formed under the bridge of my nose while perspiration stained the armpits of my silk blouse. The woman saw how tense I had become so she escorted us over to a gray cubicle and offered me a seat. Corey and Sheriah stood really close to me on both sides of the imitation, black leather swivel chair.

A dark hair, medium build, Latina woman came into the cubicle and sat down at the steel scuffed desk. She smiled and said she knew how difficult all this was for me. Tears had formed in the corners of my eyes, and I wiped them away with the back of my hands so my children wouldn't become alarmed. She explained that she had to do a screening intake of my situation before allowing me to become a client and resident of the Battered Women's Shelter. I looked at her and said okay.

As my children began to relax, they started reaching across me, and hit each other. The woman asked my permission to send them into another room to play with the toys. I nodded my head yes, and she led them off. When she returned, she began the screening process. It consisted of rules and regulations for living at the shelter—all sorts of questions about my husband: like, did he hit me, and if so, how often? Did he isolate me from my family and friends? Did he give me money? Did he work? How many times did he threaten to kill me? She gave no indication if the answers I gave qualified me to enter the shelter. By that time, I was so paralyzed with fear that I just wanted to scoop up my children, run out of there as fast as I could to my Jeep, and speed down the highway toward home. I knew if I could somehow convince Herb not to kill me that things would get better. But, my butt stayed planted in the chair as my head spun around and around in circles. She handed me a small stack of papers to sign and said I could go into the shelter that day. While signing the papers, she wanted to know if I'd spanked my children, and if I did, I couldn't anymore or I would be put out of the shelter. For the first time that day, I felt alive. The question reached through the extreme fog that was in my head. I looked directly into the Latina woman's eyes and said, "I know you're not serious. What kind of question is that? Of course, I spank my children. Every Black and Spanish person I know spank their children. The only people who don't are white people and they believe in that 'time-out' stuff."

She lowered her head as if to apologize when she saw how offended and sensitive I became to the question. When she spoke again, her voice was meek and soft. She told me to try not to spank them while living in the shelter. From the smirk that was on my face, we both knew that I wouldn't. I gathered up my children from the playroom, then thanked the woman and walked out of the building with the directions to the shelter in my hand. I shook my head and burst out laughing when I sat in the Jeep. Corey and Sheriah both wanted to know what was so funny. I whispered to them that life was funny and put the key in the ignition. I thought to myself how ironic it was that white people made all the rules, even in my personal life.

9

Sheltered

My room was on the second floor at the end of the dimly lit hallway across from the bathroom. Four other bedrooms were on that floor too. The room looked to be a perfect 8 x 10 rectangle. There were two twin size beds pushed up against opposite walls, creating a small alley space between the beds. They each had two pillows that didn't match the comforters or the sheets. One comforter was blue, and the other was green. Peach curtains hung from the two windows over one of the beds. By the door, there was a medium-size oak dresser with a round mirror hanging above it on the wall. On the opposite end of the wall was a huge oak closet with heavy sliding doors and four thick shelves where I eventually placed my sweaters.

The dull blue paint on the walls and the scuffed hardwood floors added to my gloomy mood of indecisiveness that had returned on the ride over to the shelter. My head felt like it weighed a ton, and I was exhausted from so much thinking and moving about in the last two days. My children and I put our bags down on the floor and sat on the beds. I hung my head and wondered how'd my life get like this.

Corey and Sheriah were moving around excitedly. They wanted to know which bed was theirs. I lifted my head and looked at both of them with a forced smile and told them it didn't matter. Their childish play offered my blurred mind some relief to the fact that we were in a Battered Women's Shelter. I was so relieved that they didn't fully understand that we were going to be living in this shelter for awhile. I retreated to the unoccupied bed before one of my children took it over. As I fought to hold back the river of tears, I lay there wishing for my mother. I was sure that she would have known what to do next.

I tried to calm my mind by reminding myself of the blessings in every situation. But, being at the shelter had an eerie feeling to it. I felt so closed in, inward and outward. I couldn't think straight. I wished I could become invisible. That way, I wouldn't have to feel the heaviness of doom in my spirit and heart. Also, the fact that it was Herb's thirty-fifth birthday didn't help alleviate the migraine that was coming on.

I slowly sat up in the bed, careful not to move my head too much or too fast. I needed to get out of the room in the hope that I would feel like I was a part of the world. I was afraid of my own shadow and had never really experienced that kind of a feeling. I was so used to being in control or having Herb at my side when things would go wrong. Now it was just my two rambunctious kids and I. Somehow, I was going to have to pull myself out of the dream-state I had sunk into and come up with a temporary plan. I made Corey and Sheriah kneel down on the floor with me so we could pray (They loved to pray.) I resisted the urge to cry again when Corey asked God to please get his family back together again, and Sheriah said, "I love my Daddy, Mommy, Marques and Corey."

I held their hands really tightly in the small circle we had made between the alley of the beds. I had difficulty speaking as I choked back the tears, but I managed to get out my prayer and asked God to please give me the strength and courage to care for my children—and to help my husband and me. We got up after we had finished praying and sat on the bed hugging each other. This time I did let the tears burst forth. They fell down my cheeks onto my children's heads. After awhile Corey and Sheriah asked if they could go downstairs and play with the toys. I was glad that they could adjust so quickly from one moment to the next. My migraine was now a mild headache, and I could at least hold my head up. I smiled at my children, and they knew that was the signal to go ahead. They ran out of the room before me racing for the stairs.

The comfortable living room was right at the bottom of the stairs, and the playroom was next to it. I sat on the black and white plaid sofa in the playroom for a few minutes with my children to help get them situated. There were plenty of books, dolls, and toys to keep them busy. They made themselves at home really quickly as they began pulling out the toys. Sheriah went for the dolls, and Corey had the Lego's. I saw a few children's pictures hanging on the walls along with the rules of the playroom:

Children are not to be left unattended

Clean up what you mess up

Everyone must share and *no hitting.*

I got up to go into the living room to watch TV. I didn't know if the staff considered my being in the next room unattending my children or not, and the other woman who was staying there with her four children wasn't around for me to ask so I decided it was okay. I looked around for the remote control. It was on top of the 19-inch color television. Sitting on the large plaid couch, I flicked through the channels. Soap Operas and Talk Shows were the only thing on that time of the day. I didn't like to watch either, but I settled on Jenny Jones. The playful noise coming from the playroom and the craziness coming from the TV helped my mind to be at ease somewhat.

I saw that the room was full of mix-match furniture, but it was in good shape. There was a green couch and a mantle with a fake fireplace on the opposite side of the wall. A rocking chair recliner and ottoman sat in the corner. A small oak finish coffee table was in the middle of the floor on top of a bluish area rug. A few feet away from the back of the couch that I was laying on was a rectangular wood table against the wall with a pad on it that we had to sign in and out on. I thought about my own home and the beautiful furniture I had in it and all the good memories of being a family. I didn't know what would lie ahead for my family, especially poor Marques... I laid my head down on the large armrest of the couch as the tears that had formed once again in the corners of my eyes trickled down the side of my face.

For the first few weeks, I cried everyday—all day (when I first woke up and before I fell asleep). I cried doing the dishes, mopping or sweeping the floor, watching TV, going to the bathroom, eating, brushing my teeth, taking a shower. I cried so much that I wrote a poem about my pain. I titled it, "A Mother's Pain" and it goes like this:

i'm hurting
i'm afraid
i'm scared of myself
scared to face the realities of my bleak existence
the realities of growing up as a poor black girl
feeling no connection to the ugliness around me
how do i make myself write all this
without feeling i'm gonna be swallowed up by all my
frailties
weaknesses
without exposing myself
allowing myself to stand naked before the world
standing naked before myself
believing i'll survive
how can i survive the torture of the pain from my
past
present
and what seems to be my
future
how do i express the enormous weight of fear that
burdens and threatens my very existence
my very being
i cry out by withdrawing
by living a meager existence of my reality
my world
the bed holds all the comfort i can't seem to give to myself
what do i tell my poor children who look to their mother to
make it all right for them
who so very much want to be children
who need to be children
who should be children
what do i tell them
how do i tell them that mommy no longer can protect them

from abuses of this ugly world
because she can no longer protect herself from herself
she can no longer hide from the pains of her past as if
they never existed
how do i tell my children that mommy is being swallowed up
by her very soul
where do i run
do i run
who do i trust enough to bear my soul
of this horrible weight
i know i must continue to hold on
but hold on to what
hold on to who
i want to hide
i need to hide
i hide because that's all i know
how do i as a thirty-three-year old woman merge all the experiences
i have encountered and believe there's a life for me beyond the pain
i cry
i cry
i cry
i cry for all the lavon's of the world
i cry for all the herb's of the world
who no longer are because of the expense of themselves
i cry for all the marques', corey's, sheriah's of the world
who are left with the brokenness of people's lives
the innocent children whose realities are shaped by the wounds
of the men and women's pains who bore them
i cry
i cry
i cry

I couldn't believe what I wrote. I had never written a poem
before. Incredibly, the power of the words made me want to go
home. I no longer cared how miserable I was there or if Herb still
wanted to kill me. I felt that if I had to suffer I'd rather suffer in a
place that was familiar to me.

However, that thought was short-lived. I thought about Herb's explosive temper and came back to reality. I did manage to devise a plan for my children once I learned exactly what our plight would be like living in the shelter. For one, I needed to look for a job because I didn't qualify for Social Services or Public Assistance. One of the women from the shelter staff took my daughter and me in the blue van to the office in Newburgh. There I was informed by a stocky white woman, who spoke to me with disdain in her voice like I was less than human and who looked down on me like I was asking her for her own personal money, that I would probably not be eligible for any assistance because I had a house and a Jeep.

I couldn't believe those rules applied to me in light of the fact that I was living in a shelter for battered women. I explained to the woman again that I was no longer living in the house that I owned because of domestic abuse and that I needed financial assistance until I got on my feet. She said it didn't matter if I was applying because I was a victim of domestic violence or walking in off the street, that the same rules applied to everyone.

I glanced over at the staff worker for support. She was supposed to advocate on my behalf, but she just looked at Sheriah who was sitting on the floor coloring in a book. I turned back to the snobbish white woman and said, "I left because my husband constantly threatened to kill me, and it is not fair that the rules punish me for leaving a life style that ya'll consider middle-class."

"Well," she said in a curt tone, "I'll need your marriage certificate, the title and insurance policy to your Jeep, and the deed to your house to see if they exceed the amount of assistance that a family your size might be eligible for. And if you do qualify, we'll put a lien against your house so if you sell it we'll be paid back the money we give you."

"You gotta be kidding," I said.

"No I'm not."

"And how do you suppose I'm to get all these things when they are in my house in New Jersey?" She didn't answer. "And in New Jersey we do not receive the title to our cars until they're paid for!"

"Well, that's the procedure and I need them to determine your—"

"Yeah, yeah, I know—to determine my ELIGIBILITY—so what if I get killed! You and I both know I am not eligible for Social Services under the rules so I am not going to risk my life going back to my house to get you those things—my Jeep alone is worth more than the grant. So now you gonna tell me to sell my Jeep, right? And yeah, if I do that, then I can't get a job, and then I'll be penalized for that, too. You all just keep people poor so you can control their lives and treat them anyway you want to."

She shuffled the papers together she had in her hands and peered at me over her thick rim glasses and said, "Mrs. Grant, I'll see what I can do."

I knew she didn't mean it, but I had one more request. "Look, if you could just tell me how I can get child care for my daughter so I can start looking for a job and support my two children and myself…"

"You have to be on Public Assistance in order to be eligible for child care."

I threw up my hands and gathered up Sheriah to leave, knowing I was fighting a losing battle. Before I left, though, I turned around in the doorway of her office and said, "By the way, I have a college degree in Marketing, and I can do your job so don't think you're so high and mighty," and walked out.

When we got outside, we walked toward the van in silence while more tears poured down my cheeks. A slight smile formed at the corners of my mouth when I remembered how stone white the case worker's face turned after I told her that I had a degree and could do her job.

A few weeks after that incident, I found a job. As a matter of fact, I had two jobs. My dilemma was which job I was going to take. Then, there was still the child care issue. One job was at a very expensive shoe store in Woodbury Commons and the other one was at Radio Shack in Newburgh on 17K. My lack of child care was going to pose a serious problem working in retail with either job I chose, but I needed to work in order to take care of me and my children, especially since Herb refused to put any money in my account for the kids. The staff at the shelter called the day care service at the YWCA in New Windsor to ask if they would provide child care for me during the week I was looking for a job. After that, I would have to find other accommodations. I was afraid and didn't know how things were going to turn out, but I knew if I held onto my faith everything would be fine.

I finally chose the job at Radio Shack in Newburgh. Esther, the office manager at the shelter, made the connection with one of the women who lived in the shelter before I arrived to keep Sheriah. She kept her for the first two weeks, but I couldn't afford to pay her the fifty dollars a week she asked for so I was soon in search of another sitter.

For awhile, my children and I were the only clients in the shelter. When I first arrived, there was an Hispanic woman and her four children. We didn't really get to know each other or talk much because she spoke very little English. Soon afterwards, she left. However, other women started coming in the shelter. It seems there is no end to victims of domestic abuse. The new women would help watch Sheriah and sometimes Corey if he got there from school before I did. I felt so bad that I had to leave my children with strangers, but I didn't know what else to do.

My boss knew I was having child care problems when he first hired me so he didn't schedule me for the evening shift until after a month that I started working there. I was so grateful for the extra time, but I was too ashamed to tell him that I was living in a shelter for battered women. I did manage to find someone to keep Corey in an after school program that was across the street from the school he was attending. The program was held in a church hall and, the woman charged me three dollars a day. Although that three dollars was often hard for me to pay, that arrangement worked for awhile. Unfortunately, I still had the issue of Sheriah.

Sheriah was only three-years-old—too young for Pre-K. All the day care centers in the area wanted fifty dollars or more (and that was with the scholarship they were offering me). Plus, most day cares only stayed open until 6:00 in the evening and were closed on weekends. That just couldn't work for my job. My time was running out to secure permanent child care for both of my children—because I also needed to find something to do with them in the evenings. I could not continue driving every Friday night to my mother's house in New Jersey after working all day and driving the seventy miles straight back to Newburgh. Sunday evening, I'd drive back to pick them up, only staying long enough to say thank you to my mother and to get their things together. Within minutes, I was back on the highway driving like a maniac to cut the two hour ride down to an hour and fifteen minutes so my kids and I could get somewhat of a decent night's sleep and start the week all over again. I didn't worry about running into Herb because he was at work.

I didn't know how long I was going to be able to keep that routine up. My emotional state was shot, and I had developed insomnia and was afraid of the dark. I'd begun sleeping on the couch at nights in order to keep the lights and television on. It all seemed like a bad, scary dream. I called Reverend Lewis every day crying, telling him I couldn't take living like that anymore. He did his best to calm me down for the moment, but it wasn't long before I was a basket case again.

I prayed that Herb would go and get help to begin making changes in his thinking so that we could go home. He knew we were in a shelter, but he didn't know where. I called him from the pay phone around the corner from the shelter, explaining to him that I could not disclose the whereabouts of the shelter because of the confidentiality, but he didn't care. He told me if I didn't tell him where his children were he wasn't sending me any money.

"Herby," I said, "You know it's not about the children; it's about controlling me to do what you want—when you want and how you want. Because if it were about the kids, you would put the money in my account, no matter what because they are your children and you claim to love them."

"You keep saying I need help Lavon. What kind of help do I need?" he would snap back.

"I told you Herb, you need to talk to someone who can help you understand that some of your behaviors are unhealthy and they may stem from your childhood."

"What behaviors Lavon since you're the expert?"

"I'm not an expert, Herby. I have unhealthy behaviors too. That's why I'm working with Reverend Lewis to understand them and make changes. Herby, don't you see that behaviors are learned—healthy or unhealthy, and we both have been taught the things we do? Verbal abuse is not healthy. Somewhere we learned in our childhood that it was normal or okay to curse each other out and call each other names, but it's not—it hurts, real bad—and I don't want to live like that anymore and pass down to our children, (another generation) a cycle of abuse and unhealthy behaviors. It has to stop somewhere."

"So now you're saying I'm a bad father, too?"

"Oh Herb, no that's not what I'm saying. All I'm saying is that no matter where we have learned unhealthy behaviors, we are responsible for making the necessary changes in our lives—it's a process."

"So why don't you come home and help me with the *PROCESS?*"

"I can't carry your load and mine anymore, Herb. I refuse. Besides, I tried to help you, but now you want to kill me."

"Lavon, I'm not going to kill you. You know I won't do that."

"Right now you won't kill me, but if I came back and you got mad about something, you will. I can't take that chance. I'm not the same Lavon and you don't like the new, secure me."

"Well, I'm not putting any money in your account until I know where my children are, and I don't need any help."

"Okay Herby, I have to accept that, and I'll keep making changes within myself and asking God to help me through this."

I sure didn't feel like a new, secure person—a frightened, sick pup with my tail between my legs was a more accurate description. I dared not let him know how I felt.

Sometimes I wished that I had never changed—then, I could be at home in my own bed, be in a dead marriage, and not know how miserable I was. My children would not be in the middle of their daddy and mommy's battles. In the meantime, I was forced to accept the possibility that I wasn't going home anytime soon. The constant struggle of trying to work, provide child care and stay sane became my new issues.

In my search for child care, I called just about every day care center and private home care center in Orange County begging for help. I told them about my situation, not caring what they thought of me or the shame and embarrassment I felt for me and my children living in a Battered Women's Shelter—our survival took center stage.

Most of the people were very sympathetic to my circumstances but were unable to help. In a last ditch effort, I called Orange County Community College day care center. I knew that I probably had to be a student at the college in order to qualify for the subsidized child care, but I was desperate and took my chances. The woman's voice on the other end of the phone was very pleasant. I could tell that she meant it when she said she was really sorry that she could not help me. Before hanging up, she gave me a number to call and the name of the woman to ask for. She was sure she could assist me.

I made most of my phone calls from the shelter's office that used to be the unattached garage. It was converted into a two-story office that we refereed to as the "White House." I called the number that the woman had given me, and it was either busy or no one answered the phone. I just about gave up after an hour of calling. I lay my head on the desk and asked God to please help me. I dialed the number one more time, vowing that it was going to be my last as I listened to the phone ring, again.

"Hello, Department of Social Services. May I help you?"

"Uh, yes. May I please speak to Donna Mosko?"

"One moment, please."

Oh my God, someone had finally answered the phone. But why did she say the Department of Social Services. I thought they were in Newburgh and that their exchange was 561 not 294—

"Hello, Donna Mosko speaking," the voice said, interrupting my monologue with myself.

"Hello, Ms. Mosko," I said. "My name is Lavon Grant, and I was told you could help me with child care expense."

"How many children do you have under age 18?"

"Three, but two are with me."

"Are you working?"

"Yes."

"You have to be making twenty-five thousand or less a year in order to qualify."

I let out a chuckle and said, "I do, boy do I make less than twenty-five thousand. I barely make ten thousand."

"I'll need a letter from your employer on their letter head confirming that you work for the company and your salary."

"Okay, I can get that."

"Once I receive the documentation by mail or fax, I'll determine your eligibility and send you a letter stating how much we'll pay for your child care."

"YOU WILL? I mean, you will?" trying to hide my excitement. There was that word again, ELIGIBILITY. But I knew I qualified this time. Before I hung up with Ms. Mosko, I needed to ask her a few questions that I was confused about. "Ms. Mosko," I asked, "Where is the Department of Social Services you work for?"

"In Goshen," she replied.

"Oh, I went to a Social Services office in Newburgh."

"Yes, we have one there, too."

"And you all provide the same services and know of them."

"Yes. I handle all the child care cases in Orange County."

"So, I don't have to be on public assistance to receive child care benefits?"

"No, like I said, you have to be making twenty-five thousand or less a year. Once you find the child care provider, have them fill out the paper work on how many hours a week they will care for the children and their charge, send it to me and I'll let you know how much we'll pay and the difference you have to pay."

"Oh, okay. Thank you."

I couldn't believe it. Not only was the caseworker in Newburgh not willing to help me, but she outright lied to me when I asked her for help in child care. I had a good mind to report her, but I had too many pressing battles to fight. I informed the staff who were in the office about my victory and the lie the caseworker told me. The staff didn't know about the service being offered for child care so I gave them the number and suggested that they hold on to it in case another woman came through the shelter in need of child care. (Child care was not provided by the shelter I resided in.)

Most of the women that came into the shelter while I was there were eligible for social services. They didn't have to worry about child care or going out looking for a job. I envied them for a while until I got to know more about their lives.

Jackie, who was an African-American woman and a few years younger than me had one son, named Charles, the same age as Corey. I had been there over a month by the time they arrived.

One day after getting off from work, I entered the house through the backdoor (No one was allowed to use the front door.) with my children and was startled when I reached the playroom and saw her sitting on the couch and her son playing on the floor. I said, "Hello," as we passed and made my way upstairs to change my clothes. I had to cook and check Corey's homework.

The rules of the shelter were if there was more than one family in the shelter, we took turns cooking and cooked for everybody. My children and I were the only ones in the shelter for the past few days, and I cooked what we liked. I took chop meat out the freezer that morning before I left for work to make spaghetti. (I hoped they liked spaghetti because everything else was frozen.)

We bounded back down the stairs in a hurry to meet our new company. Corey and Sheriah went over to where Charles was playing with the toy cars, and I sat on the plaid couch opposite Jackie. I said hello again and introduced my children and myself to her. She did the same speaking in a low, soft, timid voice. I understood the glazed look in her eyes and the jumpiness everytime she heard a loud noise. I knew she was afraid and felt all alone in a strange place.

I asked if they liked spaghetti and she said yes so low that I could barely hear her. I smiled my best friendly smile toward her, hoping that would help her to relax. We sat there for a few minutes in silence, watching the kids play as if they had known each other forever. I broke the silence by saying, "I'm going in the kitchen to start dinner now." She asked if she could come like she was my child. I looked at her and said, "Sure."

The kitchen was painted white and had all the modern conveniences in it that I was used to having in my own kitchen, except for the dishwasher and electric stove. The kitchen was long, but not wide enough for a table set. I showed Jackie where the pots and pans were kept, along with the dishes, glasses and silverware. After our short tour of the kitchen, I put a pot of water on the stove to boil. Jackie asked how long had I been living at the shelter. I told her about six weeks. "Wow, I can't believe I've been here this long," I said, surprised myself. She told me she was in a shelter in New York City for about a month, but her husband, who was a police officer, had found out where she was so they had to move her here.

"Really. Did you like it there?" I asked.

"Yeah," she said in that unsure voice. "My family is in the City and so was my son's school. Now, I have to put him in another school up here. The shelter wasn't like this, we had our own apartments."

"You're kiddin'."

The water began bubbling and shooting squirts of hot water, catching me on the forearm. "Ow!" I said, while rubbing my arm and taking the pot off the burner. "I'm still not use to this electric stove. I can never measure the temperature," I offered up as an apology because of my own embarrassment. I placed the dry spaghetti in the scolding hot water and returned the pot back to the burner. The frying pan was already sizzling hot when I dropped the chop meat in. Jackie had made a salad and set the table in the dining room. There were two tables, and I forgot to tell her that one was for the kids and the other one for the adults, but it didn't matter because there was enough room at the table for all of us.

After we finished eating, we cleaned up the kitchen and dining room, and the kids retreated back to the playroom. While cleaning, she told me more about herself.

She was married to her husband for seven years. He called her a bitch, cunt, stupid, and physically beat her throughout the marriage. The last time he broke several of her ribs, punctured one of her lungs, which caused it to collapse and made it necessary for her to take oxygen from time to time. He also choked her half to death, leaving her in a coma for three days. Because he was a police officer, no real action was taken against him in spite of the order of protection she had. She was also suing him for child support and custody.

"What did your husband do to you?" she asked.

"What? Oh, nothing. No, I mean nothing physically. He verbally abused me, and recently, he constantly threatened to kill me. But after listening to your story, it makes my husband look like a saint and makes me wonder if I really should be here."

"He never hit you."

"No, not while we were married. We had a fight or two when we were in our early 20's, but one of those I jumped on him because I thought he was messing with this other girl."

"You weren't afraid of him."

"No, because I can fight—even though I don't like to. I grew up in the Projects, and you had to know how to fight. It's funny, I'm afraid of him now, but I don't think he would really kill me. Maybe if there was physical abuse in our marriage, I could believe it more. But because it was only verbal abuse—even though verbal abuse can be worst than physical—I don't know maybe I'm in denial."

Would Herb really try to kill me, I thought. *He loves me; at least that's what he said. I don't know.* I was confused and my head was beginning to hurt. We finished cleaning the kitchen in silence—each one trapped in her own thoughts. The noise coming from the other room brought me back to reality. It was getting late, and I still had to give my children their baths and get them ready for bed. I excused myself and took Corey and Sheriah upstairs. I needed to lie down. I hurried and put them in the tub together to speed up the process.

While lying in the bed, waiting for my children to fall asleep I thought of the information I read about domestic violence when I first came to the shelter. The book stated Herb's behavior as controlling, abusive and battering. I never heard those words to describe a person, and it was difficult and confusing to connect them to Herb. I didn't see him that way, or me as being abused, battered and a victim of domestic violence.

When I'd tell the staff that I could be controlling and manipulative at times, they would explain my behavior away. They said the playing field wasn't even because he was a man and society conditioned him into believing that he could treat his wife anyway he wanted to and get away with it, and it all boiled down to sexism. At the time, I had no response for their statement. They may as well have been speaking a foreign language because my feeble mind could not comprehend.

Would Herb really try to kill me? No, I don't believe he would do that, even though he said it. How could he? I rationalized my thoughts by reminding myself that just a few weeks ago on Thanksgiving I was with Herb having dinner at the church, along with all my children and other families. The church had sponsored their first family fellowship dinner, and I decided to go. I had telephoned Herb from the shelter to let him know that Corey, Sheriah, and I would be there.

I drove to my mother's house first so we could spend time with her and to drop off the kids' clothes. They were going to stay the weekend because I had to work. I talked to my mother about how bad I wanted to come back home, but because Herb still believed he didn't need any help, I couldn't. She advised me that I could always go back to my house and file for an order of protection against Herb and have him removed from the house.

"What good would that do Mommy if he comes there 3:00 in the morning and kicks in the door because he's mad that he can't live in a house that he's paying for? Then, the kids and I will be trapped. We are safer not living at the house."

"Well Vonny, ya'll can always stay here," Mommy offered.

"Yeah Ma I know. Thanks. But then Herb will call here or stalk me every day, begging for me to come home, and I'll probably give in because I wanna be home. Things will be all right for awhile, like always and then we'll be back where we started from, only worse. And you know Herb won't ever go get help then, or change."

Mommy agreed and asked how did I feel about seeing Herb.

"Well, even though he hasn't given me any money for the kids, I miss him, and I'm excited and nervous, but I'm not afraid of him because we'll be around a lot of people and he'll be on his best behavior. Ma, I know Herb is thinking and hoping that the kids and I are coming home today." I smiled at my mother and got up from the yellow chair I was sitting in in her bedroom to go check on my kids. They were in the living room watching TV with my sister Fatima and her son Khalif.

Dinner was being served at 3:00 p.m. The kids and I arrived at the church around 3:45 p.m. I wore my Alorna wool blue coat with the thick fur collar—my blue pump suede shoes—a silk polka-dot blue and white blouse over my winter white stir-up pants—to show-off the amount of weight I had lost. Corey and Sheriah were dressed equally as nice. I took a deep breath before opening the door to the church hall. All eyes turned to us as we stepped through the door. I heard loud gasps and then, "Hi Lavon, you look good. Hi Corey. Hi Sheriah." I spoke, saying, "Hi," as enthusiastically as I could muster up. I spotted my girlfriend Cynthia, waving from a back table and hurried to her. We hugged each other real tight and I whispered in her ear, "They are all so phony," and we laughed like old times.

Herb and Marques weren't there yet. I asked Cynthia if she knew where they were. She said, "No."

I was really anxious about seeing Marq. I had only seen him once since I'd left, but talked to him on the phone almost every night. Corey and Sheriah went from table to table receiving and giving hugs and collecting dollars. Sister Ruby, a Deaconess, came over to where I was sitting to talk to me. She was telling me how much Herby really missed his children, loved me, and how God wanted families to stay together.

"Sister Ruby," I began. "Yes I'm sure Herby loves me and I know he misses his children. They miss him, too. But I believe there's no way God would want a family to stay together where there's abuse and the person is not willing to change."

Before she could respond, Herby stepped through the door with a large bouquet of red roses with Marq behind him. Out of no where, Sheriah took off sprinting down the hardwood floors screaming, "Daddy, Daddy," and ran into Herb's arms. Everybody clapped and shed tears. I looked over at Cynthia and shook my head in disbelief. Sister Ruby said in a low cynical voice, "See, children need their fathers," and left.

Herby held the bouquet in one hand and Sheriah's in the other and walked to the end of the table where I was sitting and placed the beautiful dozen roses in front of me and kissed me on the cheek. By that time, I think Cynthia and I were the only two with dry eyes in the whole place. There was an empty wooden chair next to me, and Herb placed his gray wool suit jacket across it, saying he'll be back and walked into the kitchen. Marques came to me and I stood up and gave him a big hug. He looked so grown up and handsome in his burgundy suit. I could tell from the questioning look in his eyes that he was silently asking me, "Doesn't this make up for all the bad stuff?"

I'd honestly wished that I could have answered him back, "Yes," but I knew in my heart that flowers, sex, or money, never changed anything. There was no way I could make my thirteen-year-old son understand that; I would just have to be the villain again. Marq and I talked for a few minutes when he asked if I minded if he sat at the table with the other young people. I told him no, to go ahead.

After he left, Cynthia asked, "So, what are you gonna do now?"

"I'm not gonna do anything. I'ma take these roses back to the shelter when I leave tonight and put them in water and sit'em on the dining room table."

"You're good, Lavon. You're stronger than I could ever be."

"Cynthia, it's not a matter that I'm stronger, my heart is breaking for my children. But I can't let Herb's actions today cause me to believe that everything is all right now—because it ain't. He comes waltzing in here in front of the whole congregation with these expensive roses and hasn't given me a dime for the kids. I bet he won't tell that. You had to loan me money for October's payment on the Jeep because he wouldn't pay remember—and now it's November, and he's still not paying. These flowers don't mean a thing, and I don't care what these people think of me. They can go to hell for all I care!"

"You go girl!" Cynthia said, and we both started laughing.

"C'mon, let's get on line and get something to eat. I'm hungry."

I got a plate of collard greens, stuffing, baked macaroni and cheese, string beans, potato salad, yams, cranberry sauce and turkey with gravy. The food was good, as I knew it would be. (The women at Missionary Baptist Church could really cook!) Herb had gotten his plate and came back and sat next to me when I was almost finished my food. We were very cordial toward each other and even laughed a few times during our conversations. I included Cynthia in the discussion as much as possible so it wouldn't become personal. My children were having a good time as well, and that made me happy.

Soon it was time to go, and my children grabbed up as many of the white and purple balloons they could get their hands on. Before we left, Sister Andrews, Pastor Andrews' wife called me over to her saying, "Baby, it was really good seeing you, and your family looks so good together again. Now, you just c'mon back home and pray."

I smiled one of my polite, phony smiles and said, "Sister Andrews, there's not enough prayer in the world that would make me come back home with the way things are."

"What do you mean, Sugar—prayer changes things."

"It sure does. But prayer don't change a thing if you don't put any action with the prayer." I turned, leaving her with tears in her eyes, and hugged Pastor Andrews who was sitting on the piano bench next to her and said, "Good-bye." When I saw them again, we were at Herb's funeral.

Corey and Sheriah rode with their dad and Marques to my mother's house. Herb still had the blue, 1979 Grand Marquee. My mother was glad to see all the kids and Herb. She treated him just like we were still together, joking around and laughing. We were there for about an hour when I decided it was time for me to leave. It was 8:00 p.m., and I had to go to work the next morning. Marq asked if he could stay with my mother when he found out that Sheriah and Corey were staying—of course she said yes.

Herb took advantage of the opportunity and whispered in my ear on the sly if I would come to the house and make love to him. I laughed, and shocked myself when I heard the word 'yes' come out of my mouth. I didn't realize how horny I was until Herb asked the question. It had been a *long* time. We had a fun time and the sex was exceptionally good—better than what I'd remembered.

Afterwards, Herb asked me to stay and move back home. I told him that I couldn't do that and it was time for me to go. I took a quick shower and got dressed. He handed me a hundred-dollar bill and asked me to stay again. I took the money and said, "No," trying really hard not to look at his boyish sad face. He walked me down the stairs to the door. We kissed and I left, thanking God for protecting me.

Subsequently, I still had no solid answer to whether or not Herb would really try to kill me if I moved back home. I opened my eyes to adjust them to the dark room, and the tears that had built up ran down the side of my face. I could hear from the snoring that my children had fallen asleep. I got up to go downstairs to read the definition on domestic violence again. Something just wasn't making sense to me, and I needed to be clear. If Reverend Lewis taught me nothing else, he taught me how to be clear and to define my life for myself—not according to rituals, traditions, conditions, or movements.

When I walked past Jackie's room, I heard her speaking to her son. I knocked on the door and asked if she was coming back down stairs. She said "no" and we both said "good-night."

Slowly, I crept down the squeaky wood stairs and turned on the TV real low. Before I began to read the handbook on domestic violence, I sat on the couch in an Indian style position to meditate and to help calm down my pounding head. I closed my eyes and took in three cleansing breaths, exhaling slowly. I continued in that fashion until I could feel myself relaxing and the hammering in my head subside. I opened my eyes and reached for the handbook on the coffee table.

The first page read: "Domestic violence is abusive behavior - emotional, psychological, physical, or sexual - that one person in an intimate relationship uses in order to control the other. It takes many different forms and includes behaviors such as threats, name-calling, preventing contact with family or friends, withholding money, actual or threatened physical harm and sexual assault. Most domestic violence is committed against women by their male partners or ex-partners. It also occurs in lesbian and gay relationships and is common in teenage dating relationships. In a smaller number of cases, men are abused by female partners, but because 91 to 95 percent of all adult domestic violence assaults are perpetrated by men against their female partners, this booklet will refer to victims as females and abusers as male. But every victim of domestic violence, whether female or male, gay or heterosexual, has the right to legal relief."

I lay down on the couch to digest and process all of what I read. The next thing I knew I was waking up on the couch to shouts of, "Mommy, Mommy, where are you?" The book was still on the side of me, and it was morning. So much for digesting and processing—I would deal with that later, I thought. Right now I was being summoned to be Mommy.

Life went on inside and outside of the shelter. Jackie and I co-existed as best we could. She helped me out with Corey and Sheriah when I couldn't get off from work to pick them up from the day care center. I, in turn, would give her spiritual and emotional encouragement when she had to go down to the City to fight her custody battle in court against her husband. On my days off, we would all load up in my Jeep and go to the park or ride around exploring our new environment. Then Ada and her three children arrived, two boys and a girl. Sheriah would finally have someone to play with. They were also African-American and from the City. I observed right away that Ada was laid back as a person and mother. She spoke very gingerly to her children when telling them to do something as if she needed to have their permission first. Her oldest son, Donnie, who was 9, pretty much told her what he was or was not going to do. (I cringed, holding back my tongue.) She was the first black woman I had encountered that seemed to be afraid of her children.

There was an unusual amount of commotion going on at the shelter when I arrived from work with the addition of the new family. The children were unruly, and stuff was everywhere. I stepped over toys and papers from the dining room to the living room. I was annoyed and tired, but there wasn't much I could say. We all lived at the shelter; it didn't belong to just one person or family. But, we were responsible for controlling our children and keeping the place clean.

The days that I didn't have to work or go in early I was able to talk to Ada and learn more about her. She was only twenty-five-years-old and never finished high school. She married young and her husband abused her and was in jail for selling drugs. The only job she had was working at McDonald's. The new boyfriend physically beat her and the kids too. From our conversations, I detected she lived a very shallow life and her mind functioned as a teenager's. I became more tolerant of her and her children and understood why nothing seemed to phase her.

In spite of our differences in ages, educational levels, financial status, and life styles, we were all abused women, and I had somehow become the caretaker of them and their children, along with my own crisis. I made sure they had the correct documentation of getting their children into school and told them what to expect from social services and where the few convenience stores were. I let them know that if they didn't understand something about their court cases or the shelter rules to go over to the "White House" and ask the staff.

When I spoke to them about putting a plan together for their lives, I had a habit of saying, "Oh, just do that," or "Just do this." Each would look at me with questioning eyes and say, "How?"

Without even thinking I said, "You don't know how to make plans?"

Their answer was that kind of 'no' my children would give me. That's when I discovered that neither one was comfortable at making decisions or knew how. I prayed they would learn because their very survival depended upon it.

I had been at the shelter for almost two months and time was drawing near for me to leave. I knew with my college degree, job, social and survival skills, that it was going to be difficult for me to manage spiritually, emotionally, mentally, and economically once I left. But I wondered what was going to happen to those two women who had none of that, or any woman that came there trying to escape from an abusive partner in the hopes of finding a better life.

He giveth power to the faint;
and to them that have no might
he increaseth strength.
Even the youths shall faint and be weary,
and the young men shall utterly fall:
But they that wait upon the Lord
shall renew their strength;
they shall mount up with wings as eagles;
they shall run, and not be weary;
and they shall walk, and not faint.
Isaiah 40:29-31

PART THREE

ROLE PLAY

10

Survival

"Hello."

"Hello Cynthia," I said, trying to hide the shakiness in my voice from crying, "May I please speak to Rev?"

"Hold on Lavon," she said as if she knew I was crying. While on hold, my knees buckled, and I slid down the white wall in my apartment that I had just moved into from the shelter.

"Hello."

"Hi Rev."

"What's going on?"

"I—I can't take this anymore," I blurted out between breaths of sobs.

"Calm down, Vonny. What can't you take anymore?"

"Herby. One minute he says he's going to do one thing; then, the next minute he does and says something else," I said, wiping away tears and snot as fast as I was talking—so much of it dripping onto my cotton shirt and the floor. "He still won't pay the payments on the Jeep and—and it's already 3 months behind."

"How much are the payments?"

"350 something—dollars."

"And what's the worse that can happen if you don't send in the payments?"

"They—they'll repossess my Jeep!" I shouted into the phone. "And how am I gonna get around, or go to work? I hate it up here! You need transportation everywhere you gotta go." The Niagara Falls started again.

"It'll be all right, Vonny. What else happened?"

I took a deep breath. "Remember on—on Christmas, Rev, when I went to my house in Jersey and Sheriah and Corey stayed

119

there for the holidays? And I told you that Herb and I talked, and he promised me he would put one hundred dollars a week in my bank account for them, and he was gonna get help."

"Yes."

"After he put the money in my account the first time, he hasn't deposited anymore since then—and he only put seventy dollars, not the one hundred dollars like he said. And—and after talking to him tonight, he made it very clear that he isn't gonna get help."

"What did he say, Vonny?"

I told Rev what Herby said about him not having any problems and that he told other people he had threatened to kill me. (They all made him believe he could never do anything like that to me because he was sensible and educated.) He went on to say that some of our friends and his family members wished him to forget about me and go on with his life because I'm the problem, and just selfish. I could barely talk because the tears were falling faster then I could wipe them away.

"Rev, why is Herby doing this? He's making it really hard for me to love him, or come back home—and I want to go home so bad that it hurts. I want my family back together."

"This is just a test of your faith, Lavon, and God will work it out."

His words kissed away the tears, stroked the back of my neck and comforted my heart. After talking for more than an hour, I ran bath water to help soak away some of my emotional bruises. I stepped into the tub, lowering my body inch by inch into the steaming hot water. When I was able to tolerate the temperature, I laid back against the tub to relax and think over all that had transpired in my life since I'd left Herb. I needed to come up with a new plan.

The reality of my leaving Herb obviously did not trigger him the way I had thought—he did the opposite. I'd hoped once I left him because of his threats against my life he would see the seriousness of his behavior and get the help he needed and work on making the necessary changes in his life. He did not get help or make any changes in his behavior. I was not back home in two weeks or a month as I thought. Financially, my life was in shambles because I still had not filed for child support. I'd believed Herb would do right by his children financially.

Living at the shelter did not make it any easier to get help from the governmental systems either. The church we attended as a family did not reach out to my children or me. As a matter of fact, they helped prolong the problem by telling Herb there was nothing wrong with him—that I was the problem.

Thoughts circled my head as the hot water tingled against my skin. After awhile, a great idea came to me: I had to move. I sat straight up in the tub, splashing water on my face. *I have to move, but how? When? Why?* I wondered and laid back flipping the questions over in my mind. Though I had no money, the thought of moving generated a kind of excitement in me that I hadn't felt in a long time. The wheels in my head started to spin in motion, but before I could get going the memories of moving out of the shelter a few months ago flooded the unoccupied spaces of my mind.

It was the week before Christmas and two days short of me being at the shelter for two months. I found the apartment I was now living in through a newspaper ad. I wasn't thrilled about the location; it reminded me of Mayberry on the Andy Griffin show—all it needed was Aunt Bea sitting outside on the porch in her rocking chair. I took the apartment because the rent was only four hundred and twenty-five dollars for one bedroom with everything included. Even though that was a little steep for me, I felt I could manage.

I would have rather moved from the shelter the first of the year, but I was afraid that the apartment would not be around that long at such a low rent. My spirits were already sagging with the holidays approaching, and I wasn't at home. Now, I had to leave the people at the shelter who had come to be my family and the comfort and safety of a place that was home. I was afraid, but it was time to go. No matter when I left the shelter, the effect would have been the same. I loaded up my Jeep on a cold winter day with the beds, tables, lamps, pots, dishes, food, and couch that the staff had given me and made several trips with Ada helping me unload the furniture.

We placed the full and twin size bed in the large bedroom along with the brown dresser and matching mirror. There was no frame for my bed so I laid the mattress on the brown carpeted floor. I was kind of glad that my children and I had to sleep in the same room; I was still afraid of the dark, and I liked having my children close to me. I gave Corey the twin bed, and Sheriah and I shared the full. Many nights I slept in the living room on the couch because Sheriah began wetting the bed.

A week later, my mother arrived and helped me clean the apartment and get a few items that I needed, like an ironing board and iron. She also brought four new tires for my Jeep and boots and underclothes for Corey, Sheriah, and me. Having my mother with me for the weekend offered some relief to my weary mind and unsettled nerves. Corey and Sheriah really enjoyed having my mother around, too. She brought her TV, VCR and cartoon tapes for them to watch.

The water was getting cold. I sat up and turned on the hot water full blast. Clouds of steam filled the bathroom again causing my matted moist hair to drip droplets of water into my eyes. I turned off the water when it reached the right temperature, meaning hot, hot, hot. I laughed at the memory of Herb never being able to take showers with me, even though I have to admit that at times I did make the water extremely hot so that he would get out. In the next instant, my shoulders were shaking, and I was reduced to tears, startling myself.

Where was the kind-hearted, spirited man I had fallen in love with? Where was the man who had professed over and over to die for his children if he had to? Where was the man who had passed out cigars at the birth of his first child and mustered up the courage to be in the delivery room at the births of his last two? Where was the man who said he would always provide for his family? Where was the man who promised to give me the moon and the stars? Where was the *Man*?

I cried so loud and long that I was afraid I would wake up Corey and Sheriah who were sleeping in the next room. It was time to get out the tub before I fainted and drowned because I had become light-headed from my body overheating—and then what would happen to my children?

The next morning I fixed Corey and Sheriah their favorite breakfast—bacon, eggs, and toast. It was Saturday, and I didn't have to be at work until mid-afternoon. Corey and Sheriah loved to eat especially when I cooked for them. They didn't mind that they had to eat on the red and yellow dingy, plastic Playskool picnic table that the woman downstairs gave us. My heart broke everytime they sat there with smiles on their faces as if that was the way it was supposed to be. They both begged me to eat with them and laughed as I tried to squeeze my 160-pound thighs under the small table.

Sitting there and laughing with my three and six-year-old relaxed me and cleared my mind from the night before, but the thought of moving crept in every so often, raising the fine hairs on the back of my neck. I didn't give it much credence though, it was time for me to get ready for work and bring my children to Mary, the baby-sitter, who lived across the hall.

One day in mid-February I was home by myself sitting on the floor opening the mail. The rent check I had written for February was returned to me. The new landlord had written me a letter asking me to send him another check because I had made it out to the wrong company. All of a sudden the thought "I have to move" popped into my head again. I have no money I told myself. *Dummy, the money for February's rent is still sitting in your bank account and March's rent will be there soon—that'll give you eight hundred fifty dollars.* The feel-good, hair-raising episode repeated itself. The difference this time was that it lasted longer and made my whole body feel good all over, like I was having an orgasm. Forgetting about the rest of the mail, I got up off the floor with the check in my hand and walked into my bedroom. I laid down on the bed praying for God to please guide me and speak to my heart.

By the end of February I found a decent two bedroom apartment overlooking the Hudson River on Grand Street in the City of Newburgh, for five hundred and sixty dollars a month. The utilities were separate, and I'd decided that I would have cable turned on so we could watch TV. I figured that I would be able to handle the rent and utility bills because I had stopped paying on six of my credit cards. I was so glad to get out of that one-horse-hick-town where the people looked cross-eyed, and they snubbed their noses up at me because of my black skin. It didn't matter that my new neighborhood was a drug-infested ghetto. At least, I was moving among a living pattern that was familiar to me from my childhood and knew where the trouble spots were. Although, I knew I would move out of that neighborhood too as soon as I got the chance.

I had to pay the security deposit, which left me two hundred dollars short of the first month's rent. People for People had paid the security on the apartment I moved into after leaving the shelter. That particular organization provided that service only once, and then you're on your own. Fortunately, the landlord allowed me to move into the apartment the first week of March, even though I couldn't give her all the money until the following week when I got paid. My boss also gave me Saturday and Sunday off so I could move. All and all I traveled up and down I-84 eight times in my Jeep with the furniture the shelter had given me.

To do all that moving, I left Corey and Sheriah with Martha, a member of our church that Reverend Lewis had just started in February. She had four children of her own and lived on the same street that I was moving to. Ada had also moved out of the shelter by that time and was living on Grand Street, four houses down from me.

Moving to Newburgh relieved a lot of stress and anxiety from my mind about my Jeep. The payments were now five months past due, and the finance company was threatening to repossess it. I finally decided to call the man at the finance company a week after I'd moved, letting him know where and when he could find the Jeep. I had had enough of his threats of arresting me and taking my sister Yvette, who had co-signed for the loan, to court and suing her for the balance due. I couldn't believe no matter how much I begged Herb, he would not change his mind about making the payments on the Jeep. Still, he bought himself a brand new thirty-five thousand dollar white Jeep Grand Cherokee, two months prior to my black Jeep getting repossessed!

I remember when I first discovered that he had a new Jeep. It was in February, and he called me at my apartment to ask if he and Marques could come up for a visit since that month was Marques and Corey's birthday. In spite of my anger, Corey, Sheriah, and I really did miss Herb and Marques, and I didn't have any money to get a gift for their birthdays so I agreed. I gave him the directions over the phone, but I didn't tell Corey and Sheriah they were coming because I wanted it to be a surprise.

The next week Herb and Marq arrived at my apartment door early in the morning after Corey and Sheriah were at school. Marques' eyes looked like he had been sleeping, but otherwise he appeared okay. Herb was well dressed as usual and looking good. He had on a pair of beige shoes that I didn't recognize, the green and beige sweater I had brought him a few years ago for his birthday and khaki green pants. Marques and I hugged each other as we said, "Hi." Herb looked at me and said, "Hello Lavon."

Against my will, my heart skipped a couple of beats and I said, "Hi," more enthusiastically than I'd planned.

Marques popped a video in the VCR, stretched out on the sofa, and soon fell asleep. Herb and I stood in the kitchen talking about our kids. I saw him glancing around the kitchen with his eyes settling on the plastic table that the kids sat at to eat. I walked out of the kitchen to my bedroom to control my anger. He followed. We talked some more about sports and whatever else was a safe conversation. Then, he leaned over and kissed me on the lips, inserting his tongue in my mouth before I could object.

The truth is, though, that I didn't want to object. It felt good to be touched. We made love for a long time while Marques was sleeping. Afterwards, we fell asleep, too, and it was the middle of the afternoon by the time we awoke. While Herb washed off, I took a shower and got dressed so I could show them around the town before we picked up Corey and Sheriah.

It was when we got downstairs that I saw the shiny white Jeep parked next to my dull black Jeep. I knew it had to be Herb's because he and Marques kept walking toward it, not saying a word. I opened the front door and got in, turning my face to the window, trying as best as I could to hide my surprise, hurt and disbelief, and not to mention the fact that I felt like a cheap whore. It was the Jeep we wanted to get before we got the black one two years ago, but we didn't have enough money at the time. We agreed that we would trade-in the black Jeep and get the Grand Cherokee in a few years—and by God, Herby got it. In the back of my mind I heard the words, *He's going to ask you to come back home again. What are you gonna say?*

I knew Herby well enough to know that he thought once I saw the Jeep, I would jump at the chance to come home, but I dismissed the thought for the moment and directed him to the day care center where Corey and Sheriah were. (I totally forgot that I wanted to show him around the town.) The tension was so thick between us that you could have cut it with a knife. We pulled up to the center, and I ran in and got my children. They were so excited seeing their daddy and brother that they couldn't sit still in the beige leather seats. The kids loved their daddy and his new Jeep with the sunroof and told him. They asked if I liked the Jeep, but I wouldn't answer. We drove out to Red Lobster in Middletown to eat. I did my best to contain my anger so we could have a pleasant time together—my children deserved that much.

Herb paid the bill from the wad of twenties he had in his front pocket, and we left. Back at my apartment, the kids played awhile before it was time for Herb and Marques to leave. Herb got up off the sofa and walked in the kitchen to get a glass of water. He called me in and asked in a sincere voice if I would please come back home. I smiled at him and said, "Not until you go and get help."

He shook his head from side to side and had a smirky look of disbelief on his face. He stared into my eyes and said, "I really do love you, Lavon."

"And I really do love you, Herb. It's just not enough to say it anymore. We have some serious problems." He gave me a hug and a hundred dollars—never responding to my statement. Shortly after that, he and Marques left.

Somehow, in the midst of all my struggles, I began to like living in upstate New York. I wasn't thrilled about living in Newburgh, but the slowness and laid-back attitude of country living seeped into my spirit as an unexpected welcome. The fact that I was constantly juggling my schedule—not knowing what was going to happen in my life from one moment to the next, never having any money, no Jeep and no family living around me, no longer gripped my heart with extreme fear. I enjoyed the comfort of being in full control of my own life—making my own decisions, right or wrong, without compromise, arguments or threats. Most of my problems were taking a backseat to the peace and stillness that settled in my spirit. The hustle and bustle of city living and the chaotic lifestyle that I lived in New Jersey just didn't appeal to me much anymore.

I was surprised that this new found freedom created a different type of battle within me. I wasn't sure if I wanted to be married to Herb anymore. I didn't care about all the things he could buy me or the vacations we went on twice a year. I didn't have a need to run around like a chicken with my head cut off in order to be doing something. I liked being still and spending time with myself. The more time I was with myself, the more I felt at one with God. The more I felt at one with God, the more my perspective on my life changed. I was scared of what lied ahead for my family, but I continued moving through my days, hoping that all the new insight would click and make sense to me soon.

As I wrestled with my internal conflicts, my external stresses were mounting. I was getting to and from work by cab every day, and it was a major expense and hassle. The finance company repossessed my Jeep in the Ames parking lot where I worked, and I was promoted to Assistant Manager after four months. A few weeks later, I was transferred to the Radio Shack at the Newburgh Mall. That Radio Shack generally generated more business than the one on 17K, the Regional Manager wanted me to have more exposure to the business in a larger store. He had high hopes of me managing my own store.

There was no difference in the cost of the taxi ride to the Mall or Ames Plaza. It was three dollars each way. The small raise that came with the promotion was eaten up in cab fare, putting me further behind the eight ball. There were days I would call for a taxi after closing the store 10:00 at night and none would show up, especially around the first of the month. The only other means of public transportation was the City bus and that stopped running at 5:00 in the evening. I would call Reverend Lewis, pleading on his answering machine for him to pick me up. He or Cynthia, his wife, responded to my cries. Every now and than, my friend Martha from church helped out.

The evenings that I worked past 5:00, Kathy, the new child care provider that I had hired before moving to Newburgh, would drive Corey and Sheriah to Ada's house. My child care situation was somewhat more stable than what it was when I lived in the small hick-town, but not by much.

Before moving out of the small town and becoming acquainted with Mary, I had to leave my job around 5:00 in the evening if I was working the late shift. I picked up my children from the day care center and Ada or Jackie from the shelter and brought them to my apartment to look after Corey and Sheriah—then get back to work. I did that for about a month, never really knowing if I was going to have a baby-sitter.

Although I had qualified for the child care expense, Ada, Jackie, and Mary were on public assistance, and therefore, could not receive the money. Ms. Mosko told me they could, but if they did, Social Services would deduct the difference from their monthly check, and/or terminate their services if they were making more money then their grant. So, I paid Ada and Jackie what I could from my check for the few evenings they cared for Sheriah and Corey. I gave Mary twenty dollars for watching them on Saturdays and Sundays and an extra five dollars if she watched them during the evening on a weeknight.

The twenty-five dollars a week was difficult to come up with all the time, especially when I had to buy gas for my Jeep before it got repossessed and purchase groceries in order to keep food on the table. But, I was thankful I only had to pay one dollar a week for the full-time day care center I had gotten Sheriah into, as opposed to the one hundred and twenty dollars, and two dollars for Corey to go there after school, instead of the sixty dollars.

I found Kathy's business in an Orange County Child Care Council Booklet that I had received from the shelter. I called her from work along with several other Providers that lived in Newburgh. She offered a transportation service at an extra cost of five dollars per week. I chose her, even though the child care benefit I was receiving didn't cover the transportation cost. I was willing to pay because I knew my Jeep was going to be repossessed soon. After my children and I visited with Kathy at her home in Newburgh and felt comfortable with her, I made the arrangements for their child care several weeks prior to them going. Kathy picked Sheriah up in the mornings around 8:30 and returned her and Corey about 5:00 p.m. I had enrolled Corey in the Newburgh School System; after school, the bus dropped him off at Kathy's house. She charged me one hundred and ten dollars a week for Sheriah and sixty-five dollars for Corey. I paid three dollars a week toward their child care, along with the five dollar transportation charge—the thirty dollar cab fare and the fifteen dollars I gave to Ada for watching Corey and Sheriah in the evenings and weekends—plus the food that I contributed to her household.

My gross salary on average a week was two hundred and fifty dollars. By the time I paid my rent, gas & electric, phone bill, cable bill, child care expense and cab fare there wasn't much left for food and none at all for entertainment. In order to pay the rent, there were times I had to forego paying the phone bill and buying food. The phone would get shut off, and Ada and Martha would feed my kids and me until I was finally able to get food stamps. Rev would assist me with whatever bill I had fallen behind on through the church offering, and my mother sent me twenty dollars every now and then when she could and also, my girlfriend Cynthia sent money, too.

In spite of the fact that Herby had not sent me any money in months and my life had become a sea-saw battle, I held to my faith that things would work out in my life, with or without Herb. The scripture in the Bible that said, "God worked for the good of those who love Him and who are called according to his purpose," fed my spirit.

I continued my sessions with Rev and constantly read my Bible and another book, The Value in the Valley by Iyanla Vanzant, to maintain a level of sanity and peace. Iyanla Vanzant's writings confirmed all of what Rev was teaching me about the process of life—through which I had to believe in myself—love myself—understand myself—forgive myself—and to "accept the things that I could not change, have the courage to change the things that I could, and have the wisdom to know the difference." I threaded all that together with the unconditional love that God had for me, believing I would survive and come through as a better person.

It was difficult at times to always work through my struggles, especially when Herb was on the other end trying to control, manipulate and push my buttons. He knew that I didn't have much money, a car, or stable child care. I believe that he thought the longer he held out by not supporting the kids, we would have to come home. By April, I knew that moving back to New Jersey was no longer an option. When I made my decision known to him, he really didn't care after that point how much I begged him to send money for Corey and Sheriah. He would yell in the phone when I asked him for money that Sheriah and Corey have a nice place to live in Jersey, and for me to send them to him.

Before I informed Herb that I wasn't moving back to Jersey, Corey and Sheriah had not seen him in two months. From the time we left Jersey my children hardly ever complained about all the different people I had to leave them with or that they hardly ever saw me because I was always working. They trusted me when I told them things would turn out okay. So, when Corey came crying to me one day about missing his Daddy and Sheriah followed, I knew

I had to do something. Against my better judgement and fear of Herb not returning Corey and Sheriah to me, I called him at home on a Tuesday evening and explained that he had not seen or talked to his children in quite sometime, and they missed him. I could just about hear the bells ringing in his head, but I went on to tell him that he needed to figure out a way to get up here on the weekend and bring Corey and Sheriah back to Jersey for a visit.

He agreed, then said he had no where to stay once he got off from work at 3:00 in the morning on Saturdays. I suggested to him to drive up and rent a room in a motel until 7:00 in the morning, and then come to my apartment and I'd have Corey and Sheriah ready for him to take back. He claimed that he didn't have any money to rent a motel room and asked if he could spend the night at my apartment.

"No Herb," I said. It only costs about twenty dollars to rent a motel room, and I know you have money."

"No I don't, Lavon. I have no money."

"Yeah, right Herb. You don't have twenty dollars? Twenty dollars, Herb! I'm the one with no money! You make eighty thousand dollars a year, and in these last six months, you sure haven't given much of it to Corey or Sheriah. Just not paying Sheriah's child care expense alone, you should have extra money. Besides, you don't have to buy as much food or pay as much for the water, and the gas and electric bills. Do you really expect me to believe that you have no money? It's only you and Marques, and most times you're not there."

"I don't care what you believe, Lavon. I don't have any money."

Herb's words felt as though someone had kicked me in my stomach with all their might, sucking all the air out of me and shortening my breathing as panic gripped me in the middle of my gut. Also, my brain waves were scrambled from the dense fog that settled in as I tried to think of words to rebuttal his statement.

"Okay. Okay, Herb. You can drive up and spend the night here and leave with the kids by 7:00 in the morning. But you can't stay here anymore. You have to figure out something else after this."

"I'll be there about four o'clock Saturday morning."

My heart hurt so bad after hanging up the phone with Herb that all I could do was tell myself it was for my children and fall back on the bed and cry myself to sleep. I was so uncomfortable with Herb staying in my apartment, sleeping in the bed with me and allowing him to take advantage of my being desperate of needing a break and pleasing Corey and Sheriah. He had become so comfortable with the arrangements that he didn't search for another place to stay. I realized he never intended on finding other accommodations after three weekends in a row of his staying with me passed. I was tired of it and finally confided in Rev how I really felt and asked his advice.

Rev came to my apartment one afternoon, and we sat in the kitchen to talk. In his usual manner, he asked me a series of questions that allowed me to draw my own conclusion of the situation.

"Vonny, how long have you and Herb been separated, now?"

"Almost six months next week. Why?"

"And you still haven't filed for child-support, right?"

"Right. But what does that have to do with anything?"

"Why haven't you filed?"

"Oh Rev, do we have to go through this? I told you before."

"Tell me again for my bad ear," he said with the smirk smile that I hated.

"I haven't filed because I'm hoping he will change and give me money for the kids without some white Judge in a black robe telling him to." After I heard myself make that statement I knew where Rev was headed and no longer wanted to hear what he had to say, but it was too late to stop. The questions resumed.

"And you're telling me that you really believed Herb was going to find some place else to stay?"

"Yeah," I said as tears swelled up in my eyes.

"Why Vonny?"

"Because he told me he would, and I believed him," I said looking down at my feet and playing with my hands.

"But he told you he would give you money for Corey and Sheriah, too—am I right?"

"Yeah."

"How much has he given you in the last six months?"

"Two hundred and seventy dollars."

"Vonny, I know you love Herb and hope that he changes. But Vonny—look at me." I lifted my head and our eyes locked. "Herb is not changing, he is a walking time-bomb."

"What do you mean my husband's a walking time-bomb?" I shouted! jumping up from my kitchen chair. "How can you say that? He hasn't hurt me yet!"

"Exactly! He hasn't hurt you physically yet, but emotionally, he's killing you, and the longer you continue to allow him to spend the night, the more you die a little at a time. That's why you're so uncomfortable."

I stood in the middle of my kitchen floor and yelled, "Why is this happening to me? I can't take anymore!"

Rev got up from his chair and walked over to me. As I cried, he held me in his arms saying, "Keep doing the work, Vonny. Trust the process."

Rev left, but not before explaining why he thought Herb was a walking time bomb. We sat back down at the glass kitchen table, and he pointed out that as a psychotherapist for over twenty-years, he had seen and experienced many types of manipulative and controlling behaviors. He explained that a person out of control appears fine when everything is going their way, but when the person is repeatedly and adversely affected by the slightest change, that's a sign that he or she might be a time bomb, waiting to explode. Herb's behavior, he stated, appears to have the potential of becoming explosive, harming anything or anyone in its path. I couldn't quite accept Rev's assessment of Herb exploding physically and really harming me, but I listened intently so I could process the information at a later time when I was more relaxed.

The next week, though, when Herb called to say he was coming up to get Corey and Sheriah and bring them back to Jersey, I told him "Okay," but he had to find another place to stay. His so-sure voice changed instantly to a harsh tone when he asked what did I mean. I calmly reminded him that he was supposed to find somewhere to stay after the first time.

"Then, I'm not coming to get Corey and Sheriah if I can't stay there!" he said in an even harsher tone. I told him "Okay" and hung up the phone.

I also filed for child-support soon after. I was surprised how nervous I was sitting across from the gray, steel desk of the older white woman. I had to place my hands on my knees to keep them from shaking so much. My mouth was so extremely dry that I could hardly answer the woman's questions. She saw that I was coming apart and offered a reassuring smile. My petition papers had to go back to New Jersey, even though legally I was no longer a resident of New Jersey, but I wasn't a resident of New York State either. Due to those circumstances, the woman said it was going to take another six months before I could get a court hearing to determine whether or not I would receive child-support payments. Documents between states, she said, usually took six months.

For the first time, I fully understood what Rev meant when he said making no decision is a decision, and we have to be conscious and responsible for the choices we made in our lives. I had chosen not to return to New Jersey and not to file for child-support when I first came to New York, thinking that Herb would do right by his children. Now, I had to accept the consequences of my choice and ask myself what was the lesson, learn from it and not beat myself up internally. I prayed, asking God to help me do whatever it took to survive until October 1996.

By June though, my financial and personal life had worsened. I was only getting 35 hours or less a week at work. Selling electronics bored me to death which affected my sales and commission check, not to mention the fact that the Regional Manager was pressuring me to manage my own store. Ada was tired of watching Corey and Sheriah in the evenings and weekends. I really didn't have the money to pay her anymore. I knew she had a hard time handling her children, and mine were just an added burden for her. I asked if she could hold out until the end of June and said that I would make other arrangements.

My phone was shut off more than it was on, and I had fallen behind in my rent. Rev had to loan me the money from the church offerings again. On top of that, Herb had instructed Marq not to accept any collect calls from me. I was crushed. I had always managed to stay in contact with Marq on a daily basis no matter what was going on in my life or what little money I had. He was failing out of his high school—one of the top schools in the nation, and I needed to speak to him. I blamed myself and wanted him to know that I loved him and did not abandon him, even if he felt that I did. I swallowed my pride and beeped Herb at work from Martha's house and begged him to allow Marques to accept my phone calls. After pleading and crying for about twenty minutes, he said he would call Marq and have him accept the call from me.

Days passed by as I tried to formulate a new plan. I thought about getting a second job to improve my financial situation, but that required adequate transportation and child care, which I didn't have. As it was, time was running out for me to find another baby-sitter for the evenings and weekends. Absolutely nothing was clicking together in my head. I kept coming up against a brick wall. My concentration was shot to hell, plummeting my sales at work even further. I ran the risk of being fired if something didn't change soon. For a minute, I even considered going back home as an option, but Jersey was no longer home for me or a place of security.

Finally, one weekend in June, Corey and Sheriah were in Jersey. I don't remember if Herb came and got them, or what, but they were there. He telephoned me on Sunday morning to ask what time did I want him to bring them back. I thought a minute and took a deep breath. When I spoke, I said, "Herb, you keep Corey and Sheriah." He was stunned and so was I.

"What do you mean, Lavon, for me to keep Corey and Sheriah?"

"Just what I said. Let them stay with you for the summer. As long as they're with you, you'll take care of them financially, but when they come back to me, you won't send any money so you keep them. You know I'm having a hard time without a car and no money—but you don't care—and that's okay. You don't have to care, but Corey and Sheriah deserve better. They shouldn't have to live under the poverty line when you make eighty thousand dollars—I'll live in poverty for the sake of peace of mind. They'll love being back in their house, sleeping in their own beds and being with their big brother—they really missed him."

"If you do this Lavon! Herby shouted, I'm gonna bring the kids to your job and leave 'em there!"

"You do what you have to do Herb."

He continued to yell at me after I asked him to stop screaming so I hung up the phone. A few minutes later he called back in a much calmer voice and said, "Lavon, what about Corey finishing school?"

"This is his last week of school, and the missed days won't be held against him. He's already promoted to the second grade."

"What about their clothes?" He asked sympathetically. "I don't have any clothes for them."

"You have a washing machine. Wash what they wore on Friday and Saturday, or go buy new clothes; I'm sure you can afford to. On Tuesday, when you get off from your day job, you can come here and pick up the rest of their clothes. Let me speak to Corey and Sheriah so I can tell them what's going on, please. You tell Marques."

Sheriah and Corey were both happy they were going to spend the summer in Jersey. I could just visualize their jolly faces when I heard them jumping up and down singing, "We gonna stay in Jersey. We gonna stay in Jersey." Their excited reaction to the news confirmed for me that I had made the right decision for now. The only drawback was when Corey asked if I was coming back, too, and I had to tell him no.

You are a good mother! You are a good mother, I told myself after hanging up the phone with my children and fighting not to be

136

swallowed up by the grief and guilt I felt. *You might not have been the best wife, but a good mother you have been and are.* I said that over and over as I lay on my bed in a state of shock, crying and feeling like I had a big empty hole in the middle of my heart. *You did the best you could Lavon to get your family back together. It just didn't work. Trust the process. Trust God. Fuck the process and God!* Oh God, please forgive me! I didn't mean that. Oh God, I'm so sorry! I'm so sorry! Please help me! Please help me!

I ranted and raved in my head the entire day. I couldn't pull myself together to go to church in the afternoon, and by nightfall I was emotionally exhausted. I finally reached for my New International Bible and opened it to the book of Matthew. I found the scriptures I was looking for in Chapter 11, Verses 28-30. I read, 28 "Come to me, all you who are weary and burdened, and I will give you rest. 29 Take my yoke upon you and learn from me, for I am gentle and humble in heart, and you will find rest for your souls. 30 For my yoke is easy and my burden is light."

I lay down on my back and placed the Bible in the middle of my chest. I prayed, asking God for forgiveness again so I could come to Him because I was weary and burdened and needed rest for my soul. I fell asleep praying. When I woke up the next morning for work, I felt totally refreshed; like a new person. I had one of the best sale days I had in a long time. I was the top seller for the day, selling over fifteen hundred dollars worth of merchandise. I thanked God after every sale.

On Tuesday, I was fearful that Herb would bring Corey and Sheriah back with him and leave them when he came to pick up their clothes. He drove up by himself in the late afternoon. There was tension in the atmosphere between us, but we spoke very gingerly to each other and made small talk. His drooped shoulders and the timid expression on his face made him look as if he was carrying the weight of the world. For a brief minute I saw myself and felt a whole heap of compassion swell up in my heart for him, but then I quickly remembered my own horrible struggles and handed him the two black garbage bags of clothes; one full of dirty clothes and the other clean.

My nerves were so tense after Herb left that I hurried to my room and kneeled on the floor at the foot of my bed, thanking God for helping me deal with Herb without becoming angry. While praying, I began laughing and crying so hard for no apparent reason that I had to run to the bathroom before I peed on myself. I returned to the living room and sat on the couch, flicking through the TV channels. For the first time in months, the tight ball of stress that had built up in the back of my neck was relieved.

For the next few days, I continued to increase my sales, earning enough money to pay my past due phone bills and have my local service turned back on. I bought a twenty dollar phone card for my long distance calls and spoke to Corey, Sheriah, and Marques almost every day. It had been two weeks since the last time I saw my children. The 4th of July was coming up, and I especially wanted my children and Herb to spend the holiday in Newburgh with me. I thought it would be a good idea for Herb and I to make peace and get along as parents for our children's sake—they needed a measure of stability and happiness.

Rev was having a BBQ at his house and said it was okay to invite my family. I swallowed hard before calling Herb at Carol Communication, which was his day job, to introduce the idea to him. He flatly rejected my offer in a cold tone of voice. I was surprised and hurt, but accepted his decision. A couple of hours later he called me at work and apologized for his behavior saying that there was nothing more that he would love better than to spend his day with me. I smiled and felt warm all over and told him thanks. The rest of that day I allowed my mind to wander and fantasize about him changing and us getting back together.

The 4th of July was rainy, overcast, and chilly. The weather was somewhat of a disappointment for me. We would have to spend the day indoors at Rev's house. I was so excited my children and Herb were coming that I didn't let the weather affect my entire mood. It would be so good to see my children again and have all of us together as a family. (No matter how broken we were, we were still a family—and that was important for me. I understood from the internal work I was doing related to acceptance that brokenness wasn't so bad because it had a chance of being fixed in a different and healthier way. I held to that knowledge like the plague, for it signified hope for my family and me, especially Herb. Hope was all I had along with the image that I envisioned in my head of having a peaceful, enjoyable time with my family in the midst of other families.)

My anticipation was finally over. Corey and Sheriah came racing up the top landing in their new clothes screaming when they saw me standing at the open door to my apartment, "Mommy! Mommy!" and ran into my arms.

"Ahh," I said, squeezing and cuddling their little bodies and then bending down to kiss their glowing faces. They wiggled free and ran down the hallway to the living room. Marques, on the other hand, didn't express much emotion at all when he looked up and saw me. My heart sank with every step he took, but I kept smiling. I knew he thought everything was my fault and that I was making his life miserable. I tried explaining to him the situation over the phone and why I couldn't come back, but he was just too young to understand. I timidly reached out to him for a hug as he stepped through the doorway. I was fearful he would reject me, but he hugged me back and said, "Hi Mom," in a deep, low monotone voice, and said, "I love you."

Herb wasn't far behind. He limped his way upstairs in his blue, cotton, plaid shorts and white, Dallas Cowboy polo shirt. I saw from the way his shorts gathered up around his thighs that he had gained weight. I laughed to myself and wondered who was cooking for him. I stepped out of the apartment into the hallway as I waited for him to make his way up the last few stairs. He stared up at me and said, "Hi Babe," with a big smile across his face. We hugged each other very affectionately when he got to the top of the landing—then walked into the house.

We all sat in the living room watching TV, or at least the TV was on. Corey was on the floor playing with his Lego's—Sheriah jumped in her Daddy's lap—Marques held tight to the remote control, and I sat in the small flowery chair in the corner, taking everything in, relishing in the fact that we were all together.

By 2:00 p.m., it was time to go. We all filed out of the house downstairs into Herb's Jeep. I sat in the front on the passager's side. I could still smell the newness of the Jeep, which was mixed with the smell of the half bushel of seasoned crabs that I had asked Herb to buy. I noticed how nice the inside of the Jeep was and told him so. There was a compass, temperature and mileage gage overhead and a button to regulate the temperature on the leather seats.

Corey and Sheriah directed their daddy to Rev and Cynthia's house, who only lived five minutes away. I could smell the aroma of the BBQ charcoal chicken coming from the front yard as we pulled in front of the house. Rev was standing under the cherry tree with the grill to shield himself from the light rain that had just started to fall. He was turning the mouth watering chicken as we approached.

Corey and Sheriah gave him a big hug and took off running for the house when they heard their friends' voices. Marques said a dry "hello", and I asked Rev how he was doing and where he wanted the half-bushel of crabs to go that Herb was holding. He pointed to a white plastic chair to the left of the grill, and told Herb to sit them there. After Herb put the box down, he and Rev shook hands, asking each how they were doing. I headed for the house, leaving them both under the tree.

Soon after, Herb came into the house. I introduced him to Cynthia, my friend Martha and her children and Jeanette. We all sat in the blue cushion fold up chairs, forming a semi circle. We talked about an array of topics ranging from current events, the difficulties of raising children today, the economy and spirituality. My mind was at ease with the free flow of the conversation.

When Rev came in to join us, he made a statement that both surprised and shocked me all at the same time. He said with Herb's degree in Economics and mine in Marketing, we would make a great team of owning our own business. I looked at Herb, who was sitting next to me, to see if he caught the undertone of what Rev said. I couldn't tell. But from the conversations I had had with Herb while we were still together about forming our own business, he expressed hardly any interest so I don't think hearing it from Rev sparked anything new.

The kids had their own conversations going. Most of the talk was around the card game the older ones were playing in the kitchen. I could hear them saying how many books this one made, who reneged, and no talking across the board! I figured they had to be playing Spades. I thought back to the last time that I had played. *Jeez, it was over ten years ago. Either I'm getting old, or don't know how to have fun anymore.* I vowed that I was going to add fun to my list of things to do for next week. I wondered when my life became so serious.

Corey came over to where we were sitting and asked his dad if he would play "card matching" with him. Corey loved turning down all 52 cards and finding the matches. Herb and Corey sat on the burgundy-carpeted floor in the living room, flipping cards. I watched from the dining room. At some point, Rev went outside and came back in saying the food was ready. All games came to a halt, and all you heard were shouts of, "Where's the plates?"

"Over there!"

"Wash your hands first!"

"You big kids wait; the little ones eat first!"

The charcoal-grilled BBQ chicken, grilled corn on the cob, macaroni salad, tossed salad, hot dogs, hamburgers and other grilled vegetables melted in my mouth. Rev was an excellent cook and really enjoyed cooking. Every time he fixed something that I usually didn't like, particularly squash, he always made it taste different. Judging from the quiet in the dining room and living room, except for the smacking of lips and licking of fingers, Rev had outdone himself again.

Everyone was full after the second helping of food. We slowly resumed the activities we were doing before exercising our jaw muscles. I excused myself from the conversation in the semi-circle and walked over to where Herb and Corey were on the floor. I asked if I could play the next game with them. It was a lot more fun than watching. After two games, I left Corey and Herb to go see what Sheriah and her crew were up to.

Sheriah was three, Sherri was five, and Ivy was two. I sat on the pale blue couch listening to the grown up conversation they were having with each other through their dolls. Sheriah was disciplining her doll the way I chastise her. I laughed when she pointed her finger at the doll and said, "Do you understand? Do you!" *Boy, she sounded just like me!*

Sitting back on the couch, I closed my eyes to reflect on the chaos that had been going on in my life when I was three months pregnant with her.

In December of 1991, Herb was in a horrible car accident. He had crossed over the divided yellow lines and crashed head on into a commercial van. The front of my 1989, blue Bonneville was totaled, crushing Herb's bones from the legs up. The attendants had to use the jaws-of-life to remove him from the vehicle. He had no pulse at the scene, but they were able to revive him in the ambulance enroute to the hospital. Later, it was determined that his blood alcohol level was 0.18.

By the time I found out about the accident—some 12 hours later—Herb was barely alive. His right leg and hip were fractured. His left foot was badly mangled, and his left hip was severely dislocated. His left collarbone was broken, which somehow lacerated the nerves in his lower left arm. He could no longer close his fingers to make a fist. Most, or all, of the tiny facial bones were shattered, making his face look as if it were burned. On top of that, his lips were two times their normal size from hitting the steering wheel, which broke his dentures, and his left eye had a hole in the center of the iris and was completely out of its socket.

When I saw him, there was a contraption with a vertical steel bar over the bed attached to two steel horizontal poles on either side of the mattress. Two thick straps connected to the crossbar hung down in the middle, looped like a swing, suspending Herb's lower body in mid-air. Ace bandages that had become soaked with blood from his broken legs were wrapped around both his thighs down to his ankles. A long, clear tube was attached to his penis that ran into a filter to deposit his urine. A thick white brace was around his neck. He was hooked up to a respirator with wires and IV tubes tattooing across his chest, arms and mouth. Nothing could have prepared me for the ugly sight that was before me. I recognized Herb by his scaly feet.

A week later, he underwent eighteen hours of surgery, followed by approximately five months of in-house rehabilitation, and more than a year of out-patient physical therapy.

During the time Herb spent in the Jersey City Medical Center, I slowly discovered that many bills had not been paid, including our mortgage. In fact, the mortgage man called me at work to advise me not to pay January's mortgage until November and December's mortgage were paid first. I stood in the middle of the office floor stunned, my mouth agape. I walked back to my desk with a pulverizing headache, contemplating what I was going to do. *We were broke! How on earth was I going to come up with one month's mortgage, let alone three? What had Herb done?* (I wanted to scream all this out into the air.) The vision of my stumbling upon him in our basement bathroom a month before the accident, snorting cocaine, dashed before my eyes, revealing a larger picture. Oh my...!

Over the next few days, the more I unearthed about Herb's life, I felt like my life had undergone a metamorphosis, except it hadn't transformed into the beautiful monarch butterfly. Herb was an alcoholic, drug addict, and a compulsive gambler. By the time I found the bankbook, a total of twelve thousand dollars had been withdrawn from our bank account that Herby gambled away.

On top of that, some of his family members blamed me for his accident, his becoming an alcoholic, drug addict, and gambler. In their minds I somehow nagged him to death, which in turn pushed him over the edge. They stopped speaking to me while he was in the hospital. (I always thought they were crazy, but now I knew for sure.) All I could do at that time was pray all the distressing commotion would not wreck my family any further and have a negative affect on my pregnancy.

My mind was a little fuzzy when I opened my eyes and saw that everybody was still where they were, except for the girls. I wondered why I had stayed with Herb so long and tolerated his crazy family. I didn't have an answer at that moment and looked to see where the girls were. They had moved over to the steps, leading upstairs, but I could see Sheriah through the opening of the poles. She was trying to braid her doll hair, but it kept coming out into a twist. At that moment, a wave of sadness came over me for her. I realized all she ever saw between her daddy and me was confrontation. If she were imitating my behavior at only three-years-old, she would surely follow in my footsteps and choose the same type of man I chose as her daddy. Wow! That was really something for me to think about and discuss with Rev in our next session.

I cleared my head and walked over to Herb and Corey. They were picking the cards up off the rug. I tapped Herb on his shoulder and asked if he wanted to come outside with me to eat crabs. We walked through the kitchen, and I yelled over my shoulder to Marques that we were leaving soon. While I got about six crabs out of the box, Herb sat at the picnic table under the cherry tree so he wouldn't get too wet. I joined him and began breaking the crabs open with my hands. The smell of the hot seasoned salt brought tears to my eyes and nose and made my mouth watery. I asked Herb if he was having a good time and he said, "Yes." I wondered if he was having the same memory as I was when we used to sit in our own yard in Irvington and eat crabs. (Actually, I wondered what he thought about a lot of things in our marriage. But I never said a word.) After we ate, we went back into the house and washed our hands, said our "thank you's" and "good-bye's," and gathered up our children.

It was 9:00 p.m. by the time we got back to my apartment so I suggested to Herb that he and the kids spend the night. Of course, he accepted. Corey and Sheriah slept in their beds—Marques slept on the couch in the living room and Herb slept in the bed with me. I was very careful not to even let my feet touch him. Having sex for Herb meant that things were okay or that I had changed my mind about returning home, and I didn't want to give him any false hopes, even though I wanted him bad!

The next morning, Corey and Sheriah came into my room shaking me awake so they could eat. I looked at the clock that was

144

on the windowsill and saw it was only 8:00 a.m. "Gosh, they still get up early," I said out loud to no one in particular. I told them to go in the kitchen and make a bowl of cereal. I was exhausted and had to be at work by 3:00 p.m. I knew it was useless to try and go back to sleep with all the noise going on in the kitchen and Herb in my bed, who was now awake.

I rolled onto my back and thought about all the mornings I woke up in my house in Jersey with the kids downstairs making all kinds of commotion and Herb lying next to me. Herb snapped me back to reality when he said, "This is nice."

"What's nice?" I asked, turning my head to look at him.

"Lying here and waking up next to you."

Oh Lord, here we go. Before I could finish my thought, he asked the question, "Lavon," he said, "Will you lay in my arms?"

I knew it! I knew he was going to ask me that. I didn't have the heart to say no so I scooted over into his waiting arms. He began rubbing up and down my back, lowering his hands to my butt and squeezing. I laid in his arms with my eyes shut tight, trying hard not to respond to his touches.

Finally I said, "Look Herb, if we're gonna make love, you need to understand that it doesn't mean things are all right between us, or I'm coming home."

"Yeah Babe, okay. I know. I know."

I got up and checked on Corey and Sheriah. They had finished eating and were in the living room watching TV while Marques was still sleeping. When I came back into the bedroom, I closed the door and saw that Herb was fully undressed, happily waiting.

I lay back on my pillow, listening to Herb's heavy panting after we had finished. Our lovemaking was vastly different that time. There was a lack of emotion and affection. I wondered why I felt like I just had sex with a stranger when for 15 years I've only had sex with him. Did this mean I was falling out of love with him, or that he was having sex with someone else? I asked myself.

"That was good, Babe," Herb said.

I looked at him sideways and said, "Yeah, I'm going to take a shower."

I got out of the bed, leaving him in his "feel good" moment and walked to the bathroom. I don't know why, but I cried the whole time I was in the shower. When I got out, I dried off and put on my pink nightgown. I peeked in the bedroom and saw that Herb was fast asleep (nothing had changed). I strolled into the living room and saw that Marques was awake. I said, "Good morning," flopping down on the green couch next to him. Corey and Sheriah scrambled off the floor and snuggled up under each one of my arms. I whispered for Marques to join us, but he shook his head no. I held tight to Corey and Sheriah and watched the Bugs Bunny cartoon with them.

Later in the day, I began preparing for work. I took out my green, cotton pantsuit with the low cut V-neck to iron. I stood in my flowery panties and black bra at the ironing board that I set up between my bed and dresser, pressing my clothes. Herb was awake and fully clothed, sitting on the edge of the bed talking, with his eyes roaming all over me. He was telling me about the summer camp he enrolled Corey and Sheriah into in Jersey City and how Marques had to go to summer school at Ferris High School for Spanish and Biology. I felt I needed to affirm him as a parent so I told him he was doing a good job.

We talked a little more about his jobs and why I didn't like my job, in spite of the fact that I was a good sales person. Then very intently, he looked directly at me and said, "Lavon, will you please come home?"

My grip on the hot iron tighten, and my breathing became shallow, as the oxygen in the room seemed to stop circulating. *Why does he keep asking me that?* Before I could think of a polite way to say "no," the words were out of my mouth, "I am home." *Where did that come from? I wasn't thinking that.*

"But Lavon, I love you," Herb said with his big pretty eyes looking like they were about to tear.

Oh, I hate this! I turned away and said, "I love you, too, Herb. But I can love you being separated from you."

We both stared at each other as the words began to register. A small part of me wanted to take them back and apologize, but I knew it wouldn't change who I had become. Herb realized it was pointless to say anymore, so he lay on the bed sideways with his head hanging slightly off and his arms dangling to the floor. I finished ironing and quickly got dressed before he could change his mind about taking me to work.

From the rolling of Herb's eyes and the curt tone of his voice, I knew he was angry and we were back where we started when I asked him to stop at McDonald's before dropping me off at work. *Oh well, I thought, why do I keep expecting things to change.* I thanked him for the ride when we pulled up in front of the Mall and heard him mumbling something under his breath as I was getting out. I smiled to myself and opened the back door. I stepped in telling my children how much I loved them, how good it was seeing them and hugged each one good-bye. Corey and Sheriah said, "We love you, too, Mommy." Marques didn't say anything. I got out and stood on the sidewalk, watching the white Jeep pull away from the curb, out of the parking lot and onto Route 300, headed for the Thruway.

Every good and perfect gift is from above,
coming down from the Father of the heavenly lights,
who does not change like shifting shadows.
He chose to give us birth through the word of truth,
that we might be a kind of first-fruits of all he created.
James 1:17-18

11

Growing Pains

I waited a week before talking to Herb again. I wanted to know what he had planned for Sheriah's birthday. I called him, and he said he didn't arrange anything so we decided it would be easier to have a small party for her at my apartment, especially since it fell on a Sunday. Herb said he would put in a leave slip requesting that day off, and I told him I would do the same. In the meantime, Sheriah made sure that I didn't forget her birthday. She was so cute in reminding me each time I spoke with her, that her fourth birthday was coming up. She would say, "Mommy, we gotta go get my birthday, we gotta get it, okay Mommy?" I would answer, laughing the words out of my mouth, "Okay Sheriah, okay."

The day of the party I made baked macaroni and cheese, baked BBQ chicken, smoked collard greens, fresh candied yams and corn bread. I decided it would be nice to have a sit-down dinner with my family like we used to have in Jersey after church. I invited Martha, Ada, and their children to join us for cake and ice cream afterwards and to watch Sheriah open her gifts.

Herby brought the ten-inch round cake with butter cream and pink flowers on top from our favorite bakery, Montilion's in Jersey City. He also brought the wrapped gifts people from the church gave to him for Sheriah, and the pink and purple training-wheel bicycle we decided to give her.

When Herby and the kids entered my apartment, he was surprised that I had prepared a big dinner. I knew from the wide-eyed expression on his face that he was happy. The five of us sat down at the table and ate together. It was a delight to my heart to constantly hear the kids saying in between their smacking (even

Marques), "Hmm, thanks Ma." Herby reached over and laid his hand on top of mine very gently and said thank you, also.

After dinner, Herby and I gave Sheriah her bike so I could take her outside to ride it. "Oh, thank you Mommy, thank you Daddy— my favorite colors!" she squealed out."

Herby and I looked at each other and laughed at our little performer. He stayed upstairs to watch the basketball game, but I knew he would soon be asleep. The rest of us marched out of the house with me carrying the bike.

Sheriah rode her bike up and down the block with me walking beside her. Corey ran to Ada's house to ask her children to come outside while Marques went to Martha's to do the same. After everyone came out, I let the kids help Sheriah while Martha, Ada, and I went and sat down on the grass at the Newburgh Library. I told them what a relaxed and fun day I was having, and how pleased I was that Sheriah was enjoying her birthday. Martha asked where was Herb.

"Upstairs watching the basketball game, but he's probably asleep by now," I said.

"Yeah, you fed him some good home cooked food he probably hasn't had in a long time," Martha said.

We all laughed and then I said, "Yeah, he could have that all the time if he knew how to act and *more!*"

We roared so loud that the kids turned and looked at us like we were crazy, especially Marques and Traci, Martha's daughter.

"Yeah, I know what you mean, girl," Martha replied.

"Ain't it the truth," Ada chimed in.

We laughed so much at ourselves that our sides hurt! When the kids came over and flopped down beside us, saying they were tired and hot, we began tickling their stomachs until they couldn't take it anymore. There was grass everywhere, mainly on us. Soon it was time to go and clean ourselves up so we could sing "Happy Birthday" to Sheriah and eat our cake and ice cream.

The fun-filled day finally came to an end. Herby and the kids were on the ride back to Jersey. Ada and Martha were in their respective homes getting ready for the next day. I was left with the mess to clean up. I didn't mind. The mess was worth the happiness I felt in my spirit for the first time in months.

After straightening up the apartment, I took a shower and washed my hair of all the grass that might have still been in it. I blew it dry and decided to hot curl it in the morning. I had my usual night time "thank you talk" with God as I got ready for bed. A thought came to me while talking with God: since Herb and the kids came to my apartment all the time, maybe next time I would go down to Jersey and surprise them.

The trip would have to wait until I could get the weekend off, which couldn't happen for another two weeks. In the meantime, I took every opportunity to spend time down at the waterfront in Newburgh with God and myself. It was relaxing, and I loved being outside when the sun was hot and high in the sky, especially if there was no humidity—plus it was free, and I could walk there.

I'd watch the different colored ski jets zipping through the water on the Hudson River, causing the passengers' bodies to jerk up and down. Couples walked by holding hands, looking like they were so much in love. Hearing the screams of children's playful voices made me wonder what my own children were doing and wishing that I could hurry up and get them back.

I would become sad and look out at the vast, beautiful mountains that surrounded the valley and ask God to help me establish a normal, healthy life for my children and me. I still wasn't quite sure how I wanted Herb to fit in my life, in spite of the occasional good times we had. I think I was content being with him around the kids, but not as my husband. The facts that I had learned about emotional abuse being just as much a form of domestic violence also added to my jumbled thoughts, as well as Rev's teaching method on life.

I understood and loved the fact that God had placed Reverend Lewis in my life as a spiritual resource, which was offering healing and wholeness. But, the problem and confusion for me were if I accepted the healing and wholeness Rev was offering, I couldn't be with Herby because he wanted no part of Rev or anything he was presenting. If I chose to be with Herb, then the chaotic, emotional, abusive lifestyle would return. Then, the rejection of God's blessings to me of being free would have weighed heavily on my mind. When I mentally processed my life from that point of view, there was no doubt in my mind of what I should do; yet, my heart was still torn in two.

One of the last things that I prayed to God about while sitting down at the waterfront was to help me speak calmly with Herb when I got to Jersey about making positive changes in his behavior through counseling. I believed if I could explain the process to him again, as I understood it, he might be willing to go to therapy for at least three months as a start.

Rev drove me to the Salisbury Mills train station in his big red pick-up truck on a late Friday afternoon. I was on my way to my house in Jersey, and planned to return to Newburgh as late as possible on Sunday evening. I mentioned my plan to Rev some days ago about trying to convince Herb one more time about counseling. Although he didn't voice his opinion, I was able to sense his reaction to my idea by the way his eyebrows hunched up and how quiet he became. I was thankful he chose not to say anything because I really didn't want to hear what he thought. I was so determined and sure that this time I could persuade Herb to seek professional help that I wasn't going to let anything or anyone get in my way.

We sat in his truck not saying much until the train arrived. I hugged him before getting out, and ran to the platform. He yelled out the window for me to have a good time and to be careful. I hollered back, "I will," and waved good-bye.

Once on the train, I laid back against the thick, tan cushion seat, hoping that by talking to God, my nerves would calm down. I kept encouraging myself that this time things would work out. I fell asleep halfway there and woke up when the train roared into the Hoboken station and came to a screeching halt. I reached up to the aluminum rack and retrieved my black leather-carrying bag and slid it onto my shoulder. The automatic doors opened, and I stepped out, walking to the other side of the platform to catch the Path train to Newark. It felt weird being back in New Jersey and no one knowing I was there.

The Newark train wasn't that crowded for a Friday night. I glanced down at my gold bracelet watch and saw that it was 7:30 p.m. No wonder the train's not crowded, rush hour is over, I thought, and the night owls are home preparing. The train car was brightly lit and clean, except for the stale smell of urine. I adjusted my breathing to slow shallow breaths so as not to take in so much of the smell. I stayed awake and thought about how happy and surprised my children and Herb would be to see me.

I was glad when the train pulled into the station. I had forgotten how shaky and noisy the Path trains were. I walked through the lobby, not really seeing anything, heading for the doors. I was only focused on getting to my house in Irvington. I walked out on the streets of Newark and breathed in the thick smog city air. I hurried to the bus stop in the hopes that the bus would get there soon.

It felt like the bus was taking forever to arrive at my stop. Finally, the movie theater came in view, and I pulled the buzzer. Walking the block and a half to my house, I felt both apprehensive and excited. Upon reaching my house, I rang the doorbell. Some months ago I had lost my keys. After a few seconds, Marques peeked through the blinds and I waved to him with a big smile on my face. He opened the door and I stepped in. I knew something was wrong from the ghastly expression on his face. "What?" I said. He just stood there staring at me as if he'd seen a ghost. Then I saw. *Oh my God! What is Cheryl from the church doing sitting on my furniture, in my house with her two children and mine? This can't be the same Cheryl that I attended high school with and who's been in and out of drug rehabs. Why does everybody seem so cozy and comfortable with each other? What is going on here? Or better yet, what has been going on?*

I looked at Marq, then Cheryl, then back at Marq and realized I was still standing in the living room by the door, and Corey and Sheriah were yelling from the dining room, "Hi Mommy, are you staying?"

I answered back, "I don't know," and then practically ran from the living room into the kitchen. I ran over to the counter top and slumped as much of my body on it that would fit. My leather bag slid off my shoulder, and I let it drop to the floor.

What do I do? What do I do? Come on brain and think, please think! Fight. No, no can't fight. My kids are out there; they'll go into a panic. Scream. No, not here—not now. Oh God, please just don't let me cry or fall to pieces—at least not in front of my children, and especially Her!

At that moment, I wished I were back on the train where I had been happy or even the slow bus—*yeah the bus*. If God could have only placed me back in Newburgh, I promised myself I'd never leave again. I just wanted God to zap me back like none of this ever happened. I begged God to take the pain away and to help me think and give me back the dignity I had before I walked through the door.

I got up off the counter in a daze. I needed to sit down because my legs had become wobbly. I looked on the side of the stove to see if the small stepladder that I used to keep there was still there—it was. I reached for it, holding on to the counter for support and opened it and sat down. I glanced around the kitchen, hoping that something familiar would jog my mind back to reality. I could hear in the far distant corner of my mind Corey and Sheriah playing and Corey saying to her, "Watch, watch what Mommy say when she come out the kitchen."

My mind desperately tried to connect to the reality of Corey's words as they swirled over and over in my mind: *watchwhatmommysaywhenshecomeoutthekitchen*. But, my brain was frozen from shock, and I just could not break out of the fog my mind had slipped into. Marques walked into the kitchen with an orange, and it was too late for me to hide my distorted face. I watched as he peeled the orange over the garbage, trying not to look at me. Peel. Drop. Peel. Drop. Still no connection.

In a shaky voice, I asked him to please bring me the phone. He stopped and laid his orange on top of the washing machine and left the kitchen. He came back and handed me the phone. I heard my voice again, say, "Marques, will you please beep your dad?" He did.

I continued to watch him peel his orange and noticed for the first time how much he resembled his dad. In the next instant, I was standing up yelling, "Thanks a lot Marq! Thanks a lot! You really let me know how much you care about me! Which isn't much!"

He dropped his gaze and looked down into the garbage can. I saw the hurtful look of my words on his face. He walked out the kitchen, eating his orange. *Oh God, I didn't mean to say that! How am I going to fix that?* I was sorry for what I'd said, and even more sorry that I called Herb. Why did I call him? What was I going to say to him? The phone rang before I could answer my questions.

"Hello," I said, trying to keep my voice steady.

"Hello. Lavon!" Herb said with surprise in his voice. "What are you doing there?"

"Yeah, I bet you wanna know that, especially since you know what I see here. But you know Herb, a stupid thought came to me that I would surprise my family and come here for the weekend to spend time with them because my husband begged me for months to visit. Now, wasn't that stupid of me to think that my husband really meant for me to visit? Huh, Herb? C'mon, you should know, you're the one that calls me stupid all the time. No, not just stupid—a Stupid Bitch!"

"Okay, so you see. So what! There's nothing you can do about it. I can have who ever I want to stay there."

"Yeah, okay Herb. You take on that 'I don't care attitude' because I know better. But I tell you what; you won't have the chance to hurt me anymore or our children. I probably was stupid, but today I graduated with honors."

"Yaaaa for Lavon!" Herb said in a voice cold as ice and started clapping. He began to say more, but I hung up the phone before he could finish. His icy tone and words stunned me beyond belief. I didn't know Herb could be that cruel to me.

I walked out of the kitchen, passed all the children and Cheryl, to go upstairs to the bedroom. There, on top of the bookcase headboard was a white, bubble vase with red and blue carnation flowers. I walked over to the side of the bed I used to sleep on to get a better view. They were plastic, but the reality was real.

Before I left out of the room, I threw the vase and fake flowers in the black garbage can and headed back downstairs to the kitchen. I picked up the phone and called Rev. I told him about Cheryl being at the house and how it appeared that she'd been staying there for some time and Herb's icy tone toward my feelings.

Rev responded by saying, "Vonny, I'm sorry. I'm sorry you walked into such a hurtful situation, and things didn't go as you hoped."

"Rev, he's sleeping with her!" I said as tears formed in my eyes, but I would not cry. I wiped away the tears before they could fall. "And, I yelled at Marq for nothing."

"Vonny, hug your children good-bye for now, and get out of there. Come home to where people love you and who can support you through this. Promise me you won't start fighting."

I didn't answer for a long time. Rev started calling my name, "Vonny, Vonny, promise me. Vonny, do you hear—"

"I hear you Rev! I promise I won't fight, but I can't leave yet. I need to call my mother and ask her if she will give me a ride to Grand Central Station so I can come home tonight."

"Okay Vonny, call me as soon as you can and remember, you promised."

I hung up the phone and laughed for the first time. Boy, I thought, Rev knew me so well. I called my mother at home and remembered she was at work. I didn't have her work number and raced through my mind who would have it. I called my sister Yvette, but she didn't have it either. I felt myself about to panic when she said Fatima probably knew it. "Thanks Vette, I'll explain later," I said and hung up.

I called Fatima, and she gave me the number. I thanked her and called my mother right away.

"Hello," the voice said.

"Hello, may I speak to Clarastine Akbar?"

"This is Clarastine, who's calling?"

"Oh, hi Ma. This' Vonny. I didn't recognize your voice."

"Vonny!" She laughed. "Oh, hi."

"I'm calling you from my house in Jersey."

"Jersey! What are you doing at your house? What's wrong?"

"Nothing Ma. Not with the kids anyway. I came to visit, but Herb has a woman and her kids staying here.

"Herb got a woman and her kids there! What? And he wouldn't take care of his own kids! That—"

"Look Ma, it's a long story, and I have to get outta here. Will you take me to Grand Central Station so I can go home tonight?"

"Yeah, okay. That Herb is a mess. What is wro—"

"Yeah Ma, I know. Thanks. I'ma call and ask Sylvia from across the street if she'll give me a ride back to the Newark train station. I should get to your job by 11:00 p.m. Bye."

I pressed the off button and exhaled. I sat back down on the step stool for a minute and thought about what my mother would have done. Without a doubt, she would have beaten the woman up by now and thrown her and her children out and called her sisters and brother and waited for my dad. I knew that all I had to do was call my mother back and tell her to get my sisters and get over here and the rumble would be on. Rev knew too.

Woo! What a tempting thought. But, that's exactly what Herb's hoping I do. Then I'll be no better then him. Instead, I called Sylvia. She said she would take me in ten minutes after I briefly spelled out the situation. I called my children into the kitchen to tell them I wasn't staying. "But why Mommy?" Corey said.

"Yeah, why Mommy?" Sheriah mimicked. Marques just stood there, looking away.

"Trust Mommy," I said as I held Corey and Sheriah's hand. "I'll figure out something, but right now, Mommy has to go."

A horn blew outside, and I knew it was for me. I hugged them and told Marq to come and lock the door. I got into Sylvia's beige Honda and thanked her again. She asked if I was all right, and I told her yeah. She began telling me that she thought the woman was my sister or somebody in my family, helping Herb out with the kids when she saw them together. "He never tried to hide her," she stated.

"No, only from me! I'm the fool!" I said very sarcastically.

I really didn't want to talk anymore, but I knew Sylvia was uncomfortable so I replied to her comments with, "Yeah's and nope's and um's."

Within twenty minutes, we were at the train station I had just left an hour ago. I thanked her again and got out. I made my way back through the lobby to the escalators leading to the Jersey City Path train. This time I was thankful for the shaky, noisy train. It helped drown out my thoughts and pain.

It was seven blocks from the Journal Square train station to my mother's job. I walked out into the cool, brisk night air, wishing I could turn the hands of the clock back from 11:00 p.m. to 11:00 a.m., when I was still in Newburgh. But my feet kept moving me closer and closer to my mother's job and the reality of my screwed up life.

After my mother opened the door and let me in to the Group Home for troubled boys where she worked, I sat down on the tweed brown sofa. An overwhelming feeling of wanting to cry again came over me. But, I couldn't. I told myself then Herb wins—wins what, I wasn't exactly sure. This wasn't the game of Life, this was real, but I was so afraid to break, fall to pieces, or become vulnerable. I didn't know what that looked like and was terrified to find out and not be able to put myself back together again. So, I shut the emotional upheaval inside of me down.

My mother was sitting on the matching couch and told me that Herb was at the house. I asked her how did she know. She said he answered the phone when she called there to see if I was all right and if I had left. He asked her to tell me to call him when I got to her job.

"Yeah, right!" I yelled. "Is he crazy? He doesn't ever have to worry about me anymore. I'm through. All I want from him is my children. And as soon as I figure something out, I'm getting them, even Marq. I don't care if he don't wanna come. He's coming."

Mommy stared at me as if she could see through the soul of my pain. I wanted so badly to run in her arms and ask if this ever happened to her, but I was too afraid. I just asked if we could leave to go to the train station.

"Vonny, you don't need to be at Grand Central Station this time of night, it's almost 12:00 a.m., why don't you just stay here, go to sleep, and wait until the morning to go home?"

"Because I want to go home now to my own house and bed! I don't care about it being late! I just want to get out of Jersey!"

My mother refused to take me. I sat there with my arms tightly crossed against my chest and sulked. After a few minutes, I asked if I could use the phone to call Rev. I begged him to try and convince my mother to bring me to Grand Central Station, but he sided with her. I didn't want to speak with him anymore either so I gave my mother the phone when he asked to speak to her.

The next morning I got up off the sofa where I had finally fallen asleep. My head was pounding and the memory of what happened the night before came flooding back. My eyes felt so swollen, even though I had not cried. At that moment, I wished that I could sleep for the next forty years like Rip van Winkle and wake up to another life.

My mother was up already moving about in the kitchen. I knew her shift was going to be over in another hour so I would have to hurry and take my shower. I shuffled into the kitchen and said, "Good morning," to her, even though it didn't feel like a good morning. I asked if I could call Rev to tell him what time to pick me up from the train station. I could tell from his muffled hello that he was still asleep and incoherent. He tried to wake up and listen after he heard my voice. Then he asked how I was doing and I told him not so good.

"It'll get better, Vonny," he said as comfortingly as he could.

"Yeah, yeah, yeah, whatever. I'm sorry Rev, I didn't mean for the words to come out that snotty. Can you please pick me up at the Salisbury Mills station at 11:30?"

"What happened to Grand Central?"

"No need to go to Grand Central now. The New Jersey Transit train out of Hoboken is running. You know Grand Central trains run all night, not the other lines."

"Yes, Lavon. I'll be there."

"Thanks Rev."

My mother laid a white washcloth down on the desk while I was talking to Rev. After we hung up, she told me where the bathroom was upstairs. I took my shower and brushed my teeth as quietly as possible so I wouldn't wake up the boys. I rubbed my body down with the Red Door lotion I got as a birthday gift in June and put on my favorite yellow outfit and slip-on yellow sandals. I figured since I didn't feel good, I could at least smell and look good.

Although my train wasn't leaving until 9:30 that morning, I had my mother take me there and drop me off at 8:30 so she could go home and go to bed. We hugged, and she told me to take care of myself as I was getting out of the car. I asked her to call my children every day and make sure they were okay.

Once I got inside the train station, I fished in the zipper pocket of my bag to find some change. I needed to call Marques and apologize to him before I got home. Herb answered the phone, but I wouldn't talk to him.

"Just put Marq on the phone, please," I said.

He gave Marq the phone, and I expressed how sorry I was for yelling and taking my anger out on him. I also let him know that he was not responsible for what his Daddy did or our problems. For the first time since I left, Marques said very genuinely, "I love you Mommy, and I'm sorry that Daddy hurt you."

The tears came streaming down my face, but I managed to get my words out. "I love you, too, Marques, very much, and I'm sorry that I hurt you. I promise I will do everything I can to get you, Corey and Sheriah back. Can you please watch out for them until I do?"

I didn't wait for him to respond. I could hear Herb in the background saying, "Tell your mother not to hang up, I want to speak to her."

The last thing I said to my son before hanging up was to be good, and I would talk to him when I got home. As I walked to the half empty train, hot, salty tears poured down my checks, and I didn't try to stop them this time, and didn't care who saw me.

Just when the train began to roll out of the station, a half-hour later, I stopped crying. I felt so much lighter and at peace with myself that I immediately started to pray: God, thank you for this day and my life. Thank you for being the one constant force in my life. Thank you for loving me and forgiving me in spite of my faults. Thank you for watching over my children. Please continue to protect them from all harm and danger. Thank you, God. Thank you.

Barak said to her, "If you go with me, I will go;
but if you don't go with me, I won't go."
"Very will," Deborah said, "I will go with you.
But because of the way you are going about this,
the honor will not be yours,
for the Lord will hand Sisera
over to a woman."
So Deborah went with Barak to Kedesh.
Judges 4:9

12

Creative Energy

"Vonny! Lavon!"

"Hmm."

"Get up and turn that radio off!"

"Okay."

"Vonny, wake up and turn off the radio!"

"Oh. Okay," I said through sleepy moans.

My sister Tonja and I shared a room. We had one of those new high-riser beds, where one of the twin beds rolled under the other. Once it was pulled out and lifted, the beds converted to a king size mattress. I had the lower bed. I rolled over to the right side of my bed, and I turned what I thought was a knob. But, I could still hear music in the background.

My mother screamed again, "Turn off the radio, Vonny!"

"I am!" I yelled. "I'm trying, it won't turn!"

The more my mother screamed, the harder I turned. My mother hollered my name one more time and the fogginess cleared from my head somewhat; that I was turning Tonja's nose! Then, I saw my mother standing in the doorway in her robe. I wondered how long she had been calling me and why she was standing there and letting me turn my ten-year-old sister's nose? Also, why didn't she turn off the radio herself? (I figured this was her parenting way of teaching me a lesson about falling asleep with the radio on. She would tell all eight of us kids, "If you go to bed without finishing your housework or leave the radio on, I'm gonna wake you up out of your sleep.")

I heard myself say to my mother, "Oh, that radio," and began turning another knob, but I could still hear my mother yelling for me to turn off the radio with laughter in her voice. *What's so funny?* I was doing my best.

I looked from my mother to my sister, who was now awake, lying in the bed with a really goofy look on her face, not saying a word. She watched me as I continued to lay on the side of her body and turn her left eyelid. I shouted back to my mother, "It's still not working!"

I turned and turned—and nothing. Lyrics were still floating in the background. I couldn't understand why the radio wouldn't shut off. My mother stayed in the doorway for what seemed like hours, screaming for me to turn off the radio. I finally woke up out of my stupor and said again, "Oh, that radio!" I rolled back to my bed, reached over, cut the radio off, lay down again and fell right back to sleep.

The next morning while sitting in the living room watching cartoons, waiting to leave for school, I recounted the whole story to five of my siblings with my mother present. We laughed and laughed until our sides hurt. That became the highlight of the day. We told our cousins on the way to school, and they laughed. We told our friends when we got to school. Those who didn't hear the story in the morning, heard it at recess, lunch, and after school.

A good story went a long way. Most of us had large families—five to eight kids, and we learned early that the re-telling of a funny story to make as many people laugh as possible brought instant attention. You just didn't make them laugh. They had to be doubled-over, holding their sides, slobbering at the month, spinning around, as if one more funny word would send them right over the *edge*. The more they laughed, the funnier the storytelling became.

My siblings, mother and I still laugh at that story today, teasing my mother and Tonja for allowing me to turn her nose and eyelid. My brother and sisters can tell the story as if it were their own—adding their version of what happened. As long as it draws the laughter, actual details are forgotten.

I remember this story also:

"Watch out! Move over!" Jeanette kept yelling from up top.

"Hey, hold still," I said from the bottom.

Five of us were looking out the narrow two-foot window, all at the same time. We were watching Mommy hang out clothes from her and Daddy's bedroom window. Mommy would make us stay in the house when she had to do housework outside. I guess it was easier to keep an eye on us and get her work done quicker with all of us in one place. She always let us watch her from the window. It was the only window in our first floor apartment that faced the front of the Booker T. Washington Housing Project we lived in. We also knew that she was watching us, too.

William was seven. I was six. Tonja was four. Jeanette was three, and Yvette was two. My brother and I got the best position because we were the oldest. There was a radiator just below the window. We put a pillow on top of the radiator, and that's where William and I would lie down. We leaned our small bodies on the windowsill with our legs outstretched, allowing our feet to rest on our parent's full-sized bed for support. Our heads hung slightly out the window. Tonja and Jeanette would climb on our backs, positioning themselves so that all their weight wouldn't be on us. There usually was no fighting among us because we each had a great view of Mommy and anything else that was happening in the front of the Project at that moment.

Day or night, there was always something exciting going on in somebody's family—a fight, a new baby coming home, girls jumping double-dutch or boys playing basketball in the court. From Mommy's window, we had the pleasure of observing it all and watching her.

Yvette, who was the baby, had not looked out the window with us before. That day was going to be her first time. It was a hot, sunny day in July about 10:00 in the morning. Mommy went outside to hang the clothes. We ran to the bedroom and raised the brown wooden frame window as high as it would go and assumed our usual positions while trying to make room for Yvette. Yvette was on top of my back to the outside of my right shoulder. Jeanette was in the middle and Tonja was to the left, on top of William's back. There just didn't seem to be enough room no matter how tightly we squeezed together.

Jeanette kept screaming at Yvette to move over. I shouted at Jeanette to be quiet and hold still. While knees and elbows were jabbing me in the back, William and Tonja continued to look out the window, waving and smiling at Mommy. Jeanette was becoming really angry, but there was nothing I could do to give her more room. Things would settle down for a short while, but then Jeanette would shove Yvette again, screaming for her to move over. Before I knew what had happened, Jeanette shoved Yvette so hard that she flew out the bedroom window in her panties and undershirt, landing face down on the blacktop ground.

William and Tonja stopped smiling. I lay there stunned, blinking my eyes, hoping to change the picture before me.

"She was in my spot," was all Jeanette said, as she lay quietly on my back looking out the window at Mommy.

I was frozen in time, and don't remember what happened next. I do remember the next day after Yvette got out of the hospital that she wore a beautiful yellow, frilly dress, and walked hand and hand with our parent's to the front of our building.

I sat in the tub at my apartment in Newburgh waiting for the water to fill up. I reflected on those childhood memories, hoping to bring my mind back from the abyss. For the entire week after I discovered Herb's sexual affair, I came home from work and went straight to bed, without calling my children or eating. My sales at work were suffering again, and I really didn't care. It was as if I had become psychologically immobilized or a zombie.

Laughter and storytelling were the fabrics of my childhood and had become the essence of my adult life. My childhood seemed to be the only wholesome, innocent part of my life so I allowed my subconscious to search through the crevices of my mind for stories that would soothe my spirit.

The stories made me laugh out loud in the bathroom and shook loose some of the thick dust balls that had settled. I laughed so hard that I cried and was surprised after all those years the stories were just as funny as the day they happened.

Whoever coined the phrase, "Laughter is good for the soul," was onto something. I could feel my heart jump start with the burst of energy that flowed through my body. I felt relaxed for the first time in a week and lavished in the sweet-smelling, apple-cinnamon bubble bath, rubbing the silky suds all over my skin, including my face. I remembered when I couldn't afford bubble bath and started to cry.

The cry was a good cry, through. I believed it released the toxins from my body that Iyanla Vanzant wrote about in her book. I no longer felt bound, closed in or separated from my body. I thanked God for all the hard times He had brought me through since I had left Herby.

I splashed around in the cool water like a big kid. The night air was hot, sticky and muggy, and I was in no rush to get out of the tub. I needed to get clear (as Rev would say) as to who I was, and where I was going. I lay back against the plastic pink pillow to rest my head and allowed my thoughts to wander, again.

Andrea was the sixth child Mommy and Daddy had. My brother William and I never really looked at our new baby sister. Somebody in the Projects was always having a baby so babies were no big deal to us anymore, even though we were young. But this baby, our sister, had something no other baby in the Projects had... Wow! What a treat!

She was a few weeks old, lying in the crib in Mommy and Daddy's room. From the time Mommy brought her home from the hospital and told us about the fingers, my brother and I ran into the room every day to play with those fingers. We couldn't get in there fast enough without knocking each other over. We would wait for Mommy to leave the room and then—zoom! off we went. Snickering with our hands over our mouths, we would tip-toe quickly and quietly to the crib to get a few quick squeezes. William would squeeze one finger, and I had the other before Mommy would yell with a laugh in a voice, "Ya'll get out that room and leave that baby alone!"

The extra fingers were on each hand attached to the end of the pinky. They were the funniest looking fingers we had ever seen.

There were no bones in these extra fingers so we would do anything that came to our kiddy minds. William would squeeze. I would pinch. He'd jiggle. I'd bend and press. We'd tug and poke, and nothing—she felt nothing. She would sleep right through it, which made it even more exciting to beat up on those fingers!

Mommy had tied black thread around the ends of each finger real tight, and that made them look even more spooky and inviting. Mommy said she tied the thread around the fingers so blood would not flow to them and they would eventually fall off.

"Ew," my brother and I said as we turned our top lip up to our nose. We couldn't understand how those fingers were going to fall off, or when or why, but we didn't worry ourselves about that. We were going to get as many squeezes and pinches in as possible that an eight and seven-year-old could get. So off we went, skippity-do-da, to our parent's bedroom to get our daily morning thrill.

"Oh no! Where are they?"

"I don't know!" William said.

We ran around the other side of the crib, scrambling to find the fingers—lifting the edge of the crib mattress and tugging at the sheets and blankets. We pushed and rolled our baby sister over, only to look back at her hands (seeing her for the first time—she was pretty), and our young eyes grew wide with amazement—there really were no fingers. They had fallen off, just like Mommy said they would. There were just bumpy nubs.

I had to get out of the tub before I slid under the water from laughing so hard. I laid down on the bed naked and kept laughing and flinging my legs everytime I saw the vision of my brother and I squeezing those fingers and the look we had on our faces when they were gone. I laughed so much that my sides hurt, and I had to cover my mouth with my pillow so I could stop laughing.

Oh my goodness. I haven't thought about that event in so long. Wait 'til I see my brother again and retell the story to him and see what he remembers so we can laugh some more. Mommy will remember. And, she'll imitate how funny we looked sneaking in the room.

I was finally able to get out of the bed and put on my robe. I walked to the kitchen, stretching my sides out and opened the refrigerator door. I was famished and full of energy. I made myself a bacon and egg sandwich on toast and sat down at the table to eat. I shook my head in between bites, thinking about the crazy things I had done as a child. I had so much fun as a kid growing up in the Projects with my seven brothers and sisters and fifteen cousins.

I remember how I was always ready to fight anybody who talked about how bad it was to live in the Projects or called us names. If they looked like they were about to call one of my sisters, friends, or me a Project slut or a nasty ho, I was ready to defend our honor—even the boys would come to our defense.

I stayed at the table after I'd finished eating and wondered where had that Lavon gone—why had I been so willing to accept Herb's name calling of me for so long? BINGO! I thought it was normal behavior for an adult because just about every female adult I watched as a child accepted it from her husband, including my mother.

Okay God, its you and me. Where are you going with this? Why did you have me look back at my childhood? What is it that I need to learn about myself right now? I knew that the answers to those questions were the key to accepting Herb's relationship with Cheryl and devising a new plan so I could move forward.

I got up from the table to look for a notebook and pen. It was important for me to write the questions down in order to come up with the answers. This is what I wrote:

1. *God, where are you going with this?* You are having me do an internal inventory of my past life, and I must be as truthful with you and myself as possible.
2. *Why did you have me look back at my childhood?* You want me to see that everything in my childhood wasn't so innocent and the behaviors that I learned were the beginnings of who I would become.
3. *What is it that I need to learn about myself right now?* In spite of my faults, past mistakes, and choices, I must forgive myself and believe that I am valuable, worthy of love, and uniquely created.

After I wrote the answers, I read them out loud and cried. I cried for the wounded little girl who was still within me searching for love and wholeness—my children—and even Herb. That night, I went to bed knowing that I was a whole person.

The next morning after brushing my teeth, I kept saying to myself while looking in the mirror that I am Valuable, Worthy of Love, and Uniquely Created. The words sent chills up my spine, neck, back and arms. I got back in the bed, thankful that I had the day off from work. I opened my Living Bible and flipped through the pages to the Book of Ephesians, Chapter 6 and started reading from Verse 10: "Last of all I want to remind you that your strength must come from the Lord's mighty power within you." *I have the Lord's mighty power within me, and I can draw strength. Wow! I never interpreted that scripture that way before.* I read on from Verses 11 to 12 that talked about putting on the full armor of God in order to stand against the tricks of the devil, and how we are not fighting with people made of flesh and blood, but against the evil rulers of the unseen world. I stopped reading for a minute and thought about all that had transpired in the last nine months between Herby and me and strongly considered whether or not there was a greater force working through Herb that was trying to destroy us.

After reading Verses 13 to 18, which said that I can resist the devil by using every piece of God's armor, that in every battle I will need faith as my shield to stop the fiery arrows aimed at me by Satan, and that the helmet of salvation and the sword of the Spirit—which are the Words of God, I wondered how possible it was that Herb was being used by the devil. I didn't know much about evil spiritual forces, but had heard that they really existed.

I did know that I was not financially able to take Corey, Sheriah, or Marques back, for the up-coming school year as I had thought that I could. So, my new plan was to call Herb and suggest that they remain in Irvington with him, and I would come into Jersey as often as I could to help out.

Just in case that there were any evil forces lingering around my family, I got on my knees and began praying. I asked the Holy Spirit to watch over my children while they were with their dad, to improve my financial situation, and to protect me when I traveled to Jersey to stay at the house. The last thing I remember asking the Holy Spirit for was to increase my faith and trust in God.

Two weeks later I was on my way to Jersey for a four-day visit.

"Do not judge, or you too will be judged.
For in the same way you judge others,
you will be judged,
and with the measure you use,
it will be measured to you."
"Why do you look at the speck
of sawdust in your brother's eye
and pay no attention to the plank
in your own eye?"
Matthew 7:1-3

13

Senseless

The night I was released from the hospital, I was sitting in my mother's living room on the couch with my broken foot propped up on a pillow. I turned slowly, looking over the right side of my shoulder to where seven-year-old Corey and four-year-old Sheriah were sitting. I figured this was as good a time as any to explain to them about the funeral.

I asked Corey and Sheriah how they were doing. They both said, "All right." I then asked if they knew what a funeral was?

"Yes Mommy," Corey said. Sheriah just watched.

"What is a funeral, Corey?"

"When someone dies and people go to the church to say good-bye and then they get buried in the ground."

"Yeah, Boo. And that's what we as a family are doing Sunday, saying good-bye to Daddy."

Suddenly, I saw that Corey looked befuddled as if... Oh my God! They don't know! No one ever told them while I was in the hospital that Herb had shot himself in the head and died.

"Corey! Sheriah! Didn't you know that Daddy was dead?"

"No Mommy!" Corey said through tearful eyes and a muffled voice while Sheriah was still watching us, too young to really understand.

"Mommy!"

"Yes, Corey!"

"I asked Nana where was Daddy, and she said he was at the hospital, but I thought he was there apologizing to you."

"Oh no Baby. Your Daddy died. Mommy's so sorry."

"How Mommy?" Corey said, looking like Herb with drooped

eyes and a hanging head.

"He shot himself in the head."

This was a lot more than I could handle, but I had to be strong because I was Mommy and they needed Mommy. I pulled both my children into my arms and hugged them as tightly as I could, assuring them that it'd be all right as they cried until there were no more tears. I tried visualizing pleasant memories within myself to wrap protectively around my young children's bodies. This was going to take nothing short of a miracle. A miracle is what I wished for at that moment as I scanned the living room of my mother's house. The faces of my three sisters, their children and my mother, looked as blank as the wall that was behind them. The mirror image of their faces looked as if they were waiting for 'Vonny' to pull the white rabbit from the hat. Not today. I was fresh out of my bag of tricks.

Once again, Corey's shoulders began to shake uncontrollably up and down as his monument of tears fall, with my daughter following suit. I surveyed the room again of stone faces in the hopes of finding my oldest son, Marques. Everything was a blur at this point and I wasn't sure what face I would see looking back at me or what face would be looking at him. In my heart, I'd wished that this were a moment that the four of us could have and should have shared privately with one another. I yearned to hold my children's faces together and cup them in my hands with gentle touches of love... touches of love that would penetrate the depths of their young souls and transcend our ugliness into beauty.

I would have given anything to replace our reality with that picture, but what life held for us was a funeral to prepare for on Sunday. A funeral where there would be flowers of a bleeding heart at the head of the coffin which would contain the dead body of their Daddy—my husband.

I had never thought that day would come so soon in my young life. To be a widow was for older people, people who have lived long enough to grow old together, or at least older than thirty-four. There was no one to ask how I was supposed to act or what to say. Should I smile? Maybe, but not too much. Should I laugh? Cry?

Shout? What? What does a widow do?

There was no one there to hold me or guide me through my own confusion, and I was too afraid to expose my vulnerable state... afraid my family wouldn't understand. Frankly, I didn't trust anybody with my well being so I chose to go it alone, believing God would give me the strength to get through.

I remember thinking if Herb died before me, how sad I would be, how much I would cry, how much I would miss him, and how distraught I would be. All the people would be at the house—our house, offering their sympathy of support. They would be crying; laughing; staring; shaking their heads; sleeping; playing; screaming; and eating the collard greens that are flavored with smoked turkey, beans, ham, salads, chicken, baked macaroni and cheese, cakes, pies, soda, and beer. I would be hearing all the "I'm sorry's" and "I can't believe its" and all the other things people say when someone dies. But, none of that happened for me. I was cheated out of all those dying details and so were my children. We were cheated because his family and some of our friends couldn't accept the horrid fact that Herb was the one who pointed the gun at my head, pulled the trigger six times and then reloaded to shoot a bullet in his own head and committing suicide.

In spite of the fact that my in-laws and I had had a strained relationship (We had tolerated each other over the sixteen years.) their blaming me for Herb's death didn't justify them staying away from my children and not calling to see how they were doing. How was I supposed to cope with that reality? Also, how would I explain their behavior to my children?

To this day I don't know for sure how much any of my children remembers about the shooting, much less how it's going to affect their lives. I'm sure as time goes by, though, they will come to me for answers to their questions.

But right then, I was afraid... afraid to think of what life held for us as a wounded family. Where there had once been five of us in the car—five at the dinner table—five in the pictures—five lying around the living room, now there were only four. Now, I was the only adult left who could offer love, support, strength, and security for my children in the midst of everyone's tragic loss.

The next day after being released from the hospital, there was so much to do. With the broken foot and the staples still in my stomach, my movements were very limited. I needed the crutches to get around, and that really slowed me down. I didn't want anybody to do anything. I felt that I should do the final arrangements for saying good-bye to Herb. No matter what had happened, he was my husband, and I knew I still loved him, even though emotionally I couldn't feel a thing. I needed to know that I did all I could for him in death just as I had done for him in life.

Oh, flowers. I gotta buy flowers. What kind of flowers am I supposed to buy? Don't know. The flower shop man—he'll know. Maybe when I go buy the flowers, the reality of Herb's funeral will sink in, knowing that this is going to be the end of whatever we had together. I have no money. Mommy will loan me some I'm sure—just as she has had to loan me her red sweat suit I have on now.

My mother took me to the florist on Bergen Avenue and dropped me off while she found a place to park. I went into the flower shop and asked the florist what kind of flowers do you buy for a funeral. He handed me a book with all kinds of flowers in it for funerals and asked me if I was the wife. I said, "Yes."

He recommended the bleeding heart because traditionally that's what widows purchased for their husbands' funerals. I knew the choice I would make, but I looked through the entire book anyway because I yearned for something to cleanse me like a cool breeze on a hot humid summer night.

The experience of standing in the flower shop, and looking at the picture of the bleeding heart that consisted of an array of white carnation flowers with red carnations flowing down the center to represent the blood struck me at the core of my sorrow. Once again, though, I was adding another blood-boiling episode to my already overflowing teakettle of emotions. I knew if this pent-up frustration continued I would burst like a river dam out of control, and destroy everything in my path, including me. I needed to cry, shout, kick, or scream... anything to let go of all the hurt and anger so I could feel the grief that apparently was building in my heart.

176

14

Spiritual Armor

My thoughts were drawn back to the morning of the shooting as I sat on my mother's striped, chase lounge sofa. *Lord have mercy!* I only went upstairs to look for barrettes for my daughter's hair, never believing that Herb would point a gun to my head and pull the trigger. If only I could have seen his eyes for "The eyes are the windows of the soul."

POW! That was all I heard. Then, I felt death and the bullet flowing through my body at the same pace. I was frozen in time, waiting to die, but my spirit completely trusted and believed that God would spare my life if I only asked. At that very moment, I was somehow transported to this spiritual realm for what felt like an eternity as the slowness of death was claiming my life. My spirit prayed, asking God to please not take me yet because I had too much to do.

Instantly, what felt like a bolt of light struck me in the top of my head, jolting my body to the right, returning life back to my body and stopping the bullet on the right side of my head. *Oh my God! I am not dead yet!* Upon that realization, I immediately ran past my husband, bolting out the bedroom door to the stairs. I felt a ping in my butt, and from a standing position, I dove down the steep stairs. It was as if a spiritual force had covered my whole body like a protective shield. When I opened my eyes, I was stretched out on the stairs, with my left hand pressing against the left side of my head where the bullet had entered. I pushed myself down the stairs with the backs of my feet and my right arm. I felt the presence of the spiritual force underneath me like a cushion, holding the sides of my head steady, guiding me evenly down the steps.

When I reached the bottom of the stairs, I crawled under my oldest son's arm and around the banister into the living room. I jumped up from the rose-colored carpeted floor, yelling for my children to run. I saw that Marques was still standing by the banister with his right arm stretched out and his hand holding tight to the top part. He looked like he was in shock. I ran to him and shook him frantically, yelling at him to run. Corey and Sheriah ran to me and saw the blood dipping from my hair. I begged them not to cry, to please just run. The four of us ran together, heading for the backdoor in the kitchen. *Oh Lord; please let this door open this time without sticking!* Marques unlocked the door, took the chain off and pulled it open. We all ran out of the house, down the driveway.

It wasn't until days later while I was in the hospital that I learned Herby had reloaded the gun after shooting all six bullets. Four were in me, one went into the wall to the right past Sheriah's head and the other one went into the front door, just grazing past Marques' left shoulder.

Herby did not shoot himself right away as I had thought. According to Marques and a neighbor who watched him from her bedroom window, he came outside onto the porch with his hands in his pockets, looking around. Marques saw his dad standing there watching us run. They gazed into each other's eyes from across the street as Marques desperately rang Sylvia's doorbell. Then, he came down off the porch and started walking in the direction of the house where the kids and I were. Once he saw the police car drive up to the house, he turned around, heading back toward our house. The police gave chase, but couldn't find him. He went through the back door, the same door the kids and I had run out of. By the time the police found him in the dining room, his head was lying on an umbrella where all the blood from the gunshot had gushed out. But, he wasn't dead yet.

I sat on my mother's sofa thinking about all that and how tragically my life had changed in a blink of an eye. If it weren't for the four bullet wounds, the thirty-three staples in my stomach, the cast on my broken foot, and Herb's funeral that I still had to attend, I would not have believed it. I was really thankful that it was 5:00 in the morning and no one was up yet. I still had another two hours of peace and quiet before I had to put on the strong front for my children and everyone else who was having a hard time believing what had happened.

The Lord is my shepherd;
I shall not want.
He maketh me to lie down in green pastures:
he leadeth me beside the still waters.
He restoreth my soul:
he leadeth me in the paths of righteousness
for his name's sake.
Yea, though I walk through the
valley of the shadow of death,
I will fear no evil: for thou art with me;
thy rod and thy staff they comfort me.
Thou preparest a table before me
in the presence of mine enemies:
thou anointest my head with oil;
my cup runneth over.
Surely goodness and mercy shall follow me
all the days of my life:
and I will dwell in the house of
the Lord for ever.
Psalm 23

15

The Funeral

I wanted a bath! I woke up the morning of the funeral determined that a bath was what I was going to have. I had not taken a shower in over a week and was tired of those sponge baths. I needed to figure out a way of not getting the cast on my foot completely wet—not to mention the staples that were still in my stomach. My hair was smelly from all the blood and needed washing badly, too.

My mother came up with a great idea after I told her my dilemma. She suggested that I wrap the leg with the cast in a large garbage bag, tying the ends and hanging that leg over the side of the tub. We both laughed at the thought of that sight, but it was a workable plan. All I needed now was someone to help get me in and out of the tub and wash my hair and body.

I called my friend Mrs. Davenport. She used to work as a home aide attendant for the elderly, and she was also a beautician at Candies Hair Artistry—her daughter's shop in Jersey City. Mrs. Davenport shampooed my hair most of the time I went in the shop while I still lived in New Jersey. We engaged in empowering conversations about God. After awhile, we became good friends. In fact, she was one of the few people who genuinely reached out to me during my whole ordeal.

Mrs. Davenport came over to my mother's one bedroom apartment with her warm friendly smile, so happy that I called. I had not seen or talked to her the entire time I'd been gone. Her presence was a breath of fresh air. We exchanged hugs and embraced for a long time. The tears flowed freely from my eyes, streaming down my cheeks and landing on the shoulder of her white, cotton blouse. I knew she understood all the pain behind the tears from the way she held me tighter and tighter with each sob.

We walked to the bathroom, and I got undressed as Mrs. Davenport tested the temperature of the water. She helped lower me into the tub, making sure that the leg with the cast and plastic bag hung over the side. The hot water running down my neck, back and breasts was so soothing to my tense muscles. I wished that I could have stayed in the tub for the rest of my life and hidden from the world. I especially wanted the events of the day to pass me by.

Mrs. Davenport washed my body very gently and lovingly, being extremely careful not to wet the bandages covering my stomach. I felt myself beginning to relax with each touch, almost believing all that had happened was just a bad dream until she began pouring the water in my hair. Blood mixed with dirt started running down into the water. There was so much blood. It filled the front of the tub. Thank God we just let the water run into the tub without plugging it up. I pretended seeing all the blood was no big deal and continued to talk about how great it was to finally take a bath. But, once she put the creamy white shampoo in my hair, there was no more pretending. The shampoo turned dirty red within seconds. Reality was back. Herb had shot me in the head, and I was going to his funeral some several hours later.

Somehow, Mrs. Davenport washed my body and my hair without getting my cast or staples wet. She then helped me out of the tub and proceeded to dry me off, assuring me in her soothing voice that God loved me and would continue to shine His grace down upon me and protect and comfort me from whatever was to come. For a brief moment, I felt like a different person.

As time drew near, my family kept asking me if I was all right. "Yes I am!" I would say with an increasingly agitated tone, and they would just glare at me with that unbelieving look. I didn't care. I wanted everybody to go away and stop watching me as if I was going to do something bizarre.

I wanted to scream that it was weird preparing to go to my husband's funeral wearing my mother's big black and white dress— and my sister Yvette's black and white hat with a black net attached to the front—making me look like the grieving widow; when I was only supposed to be here on a four day visit. But, I dared not because I knew their questions were out of love and concern for me. What did it matter? My screaming at them wouldn't change a thing.

I eyed my children who looked so handsome and pretty sitting on the stripe couch, waiting patiently for my command. Anybody would have thought they were going to a happy-occasion-function. My heart began to pit-a-patta at the thought of them witnessing the shooting and seeing their daddy in a coffin. I thought the throbbing pulse would cause my stapled stomach to burst at any minute. *How much more?* That's all I heard myself saying in my head as I sat there pondering my next move.

I asked my children for the third time if they were all right. I needed to hear their innocent reassurance so that I'd feel all right too, knowing that I wasn't. A few minutes later, we left the house and got into Herb's brand new white Jeep Grand Cherokee with my mother in the driver's seat taking us to Missionary Baptist Church.

The church was about ten or fifteen minutes away from my mother's house, between Bright Street and Jersey Avenue. Herb and I were married there over ten years ago. During that time, he had become a Deacon and I was a Deaconess—other than that, not much about the church had changed, including the people.

The front of the church is surrounded with black iron gates and three wide gray concrete steps leading up to the double triangular doors. It has a high steeple roof with a black steel cross at the peek. A clock is recessed just below the peak, and the church is centered among brownstone apartment buildings. As a matter of fact, the building Herb grew up in is attached to the church and is owned by the church.

Pastor Andrews was still the pastor, even though he had become very sick over the past few years. About twenty-five to thirty members attended service regularly with their children. The same industrial red carpet with black specks covered the floor. There were stain glass windows along the side of the walls and about twenty long rows of wooden pews on either side of the center aisle. In the front of the church sat a square, mahogany wooden table with a thick, golden, five-inch cross in the middle. The table would not be there for the funeral, instead Herb's coffin would. Next, was the pulpit. It was elevated like a stage with the red and black specked carpet. There were three high back wooden chairs that rested against the low wall of the pulpit and an angular three-foot podium that held the Holy Bible. Directly behind the pulpit was the choir section. It was sloped a few feet above the pulpit and offered the best view of the church. There were four rows that contained eight to ten wooden folding chairs. Over to the left sat the new black baby grand piano the church purchased the summer before I left.

My mother dropped my children and I off across the street from the church. She had to find a place to park. When I saw the millions of people standing outside of the church, I was overcome with grief and slumped over my crutches. My Uncle Sonny (Aunt Barbara Ann's husband), who was standing out front by the door, saw me and ran over to help me. He held me in his arms until someone came with a wheelchair. My uncle handed my crutches to Marques before helping me in the wheelchair. He bent down and wiped my tears away and said he loved me and that everything would be all right. He wheeled me across the street and into the church as my children walked along side of us with frightened expressions on their faces.

The church was just as packed. I felt all eyes were on me as my uncle rolled me down the center aisle. The Choir was already in the stand when we entered. The Deacons and Deaconess were seated off to the left of the center aisle in their traditional white attire. The pastors that had attended (including Reverend Lewis) were seated in the pulpit with a few additional chairs. I asked myself who were all these people? Where did they come from? Had Herb and I known this many people?

My uncle parked me by the front pew and went to take his seat a few rows back. The respectful mourners' eyes were now burning a hole in the back of my head. I looked straight ahead at the coffin that held the dead body of my husband in an effort not to meet anybody's eyes. Marques slid as close to me as he could and begged me to let him leave and go outside because he couldn't handle his grief. Reluctantly, I said yes, because I knew I wanted to leave, too. Feeling like a source of strength and protection was gone, my inner security began to slowly wither, but I knew my Uncle Sonny and my mother were close by.

Sheriah was sitting with my sister Yvette and her daughter, Brittany. Yvette took the girls to look at Herb. Sheriah yelled out in her four-year-old way, "My Daddy's sleeping." My heart almost split in two when I heard her. Corey was sitting to the right of me in the front row looking like the happy-go-lucky kid that he is. I knew he would stay close by me. One of his friends came and joined him in the front row and they talked about whatever seven-year-old boys talk about. Sheriah on the other hand, found it a great thrill to keep having my sister take her to look at her daddy sleeping. My two younger children's attitude and behavior gave me comfort. But Marques I worried about.

Neither Marques nor I had shown any emotion from the time of the shooting until now. I knew he must have been feeling as numb as I was so that he could protect himself from the reality of all that had taken place. There wasn't a thing I could do to help break through the darkness of his deadened senses, for my own were worse off. I couldn't even smell the many flowers that were no more than five feet away from me. My eyes were very blurry, barely able to focus on what was in front of me. My ears rendered me a deaf-mute. Everything I touched felt plastic; my mouth tasted like stale cardboard, and I wouldn't see Marques again until after the funeral when we were in the church hall.

Herb's brother and three sisters sat in the front row also. (One sister was not present.) We barely exchanged looks or conversation during the service. The rest of his family and my family were intermingled throughout the pews. The tension among our families reminded me of the Hatfields and McCoy's.

As large as the church was and as many people as there were, you could hear a pin drop when my Uncle Sonny wheeled me to

Herb's coffin to take a final view of him before the funeral attendants closed the casket. I was assisted out of the wheelchair by my elbows and stood up on my crutches to see my husband. It sounded as if everybody held their breaths as I looked down into the casket at the dull, stiff body. I quickly surveyed the side of his head for the bullet wound, but it wasn't visible. *Thank God.* Then, I touched his cold hands and one tear from each eye rolled down my cheeks. I turned from the coffin with the assistance of my uncle supporting me by the arms. He eased me back into the wheelchair and pushed me back to my spot.

The Choir began singing, breaking the deadly silence in the church. Someone read the obituary. Reverend Lewis sang a solo that I'd requested of him earlier, 'Don't Let My Living Be In Vain'—another solo was sung by a friend of the family, and Pastor Poll, the Assistant Pastor, preached a sermon about 'We Are Family'.

I sat through the entire funeral with a blank look on my face and a hole so deep within my heart that it could have been Herb's burial ground.

16

Mirror Images

The woman in the mirror remembers a lot of what the little girl felt like and said at age thirteen. She remembers the little girl feeling special in the way she thought and carried herself. She remembers her special relationship with God. She remembers not knowing how she knew she could trust God and talk to Him, but she did anyhow, always feeling safe, secure, protected and loved.

Going to God than was as special a time and place for her as it is tonight. (Her relationship with God was her secret. Secrets that no one could take away and make fun of or make her feel dirty and ashamed.) So, as the woman watches herself in the glass feeling those special feelings of old, she's astonished as the tears of a thirteen-year-old girl begin rolling down her cheeks. The woman sees another person's face looking back at her in the mirror—the reflection and feelings of a little girl searching for love.

The woman has attained so much from the girl. She has encountered a great spiritual love through the aid of the child, but has finally had to accept the reality that the love she's come to know with Herb cannot be experienced to its full potential. So, she goes back to her special place with God, wrapped in His arms crying for what can't ever be.

When I was thirteen, my parents separated due to the arguing and fighting, and suddenly, they were getting a divorce. My world was shattered, I was afraid and felt so alone. Although my understanding of who God was in my life at thirteen was very limited, the presence of His love was comforting. I didn't know where that feeling came from or why it was there, but I gravitated to it.

My brothers and sisters and I didn't have a deep religious or spiritual upbringing. We weren't made to go to church every Sunday or sit around the kitchen table for family discussions about the importance of having God in our lives. We were not Baptists like so many others in the Projects. As a matter of fact, we were one of the few African-American families that were Catholic—with the exception of all my cousins and Grandmother.

We all attended St. Bridget's Grammar School and went to Mass the first Friday of the month. We made our Communion, Confirmation, and went to confession. Once and awhile, some of us would walk the fifteen blocks to St. Bridget's Church on Sunday and attend Mass, or sometimes I would go by myself. That was the extent of my relationship with God, and I thought that was all it was supposed to be. It wasn't until I was twenty-six that I made a conscious decision to seek God's guidance and find out if there was any more to this 'God' I kept hearing about.

I was at home a month after I had given birth to Corey, sitting on my beige and brown speckled couch with my weary legs stretched out. Corey was lying in his baby seat on the rose colored carpet. My childhood friend Bertha Bobo had died two weeks before Corey's birth of cardiac arrest, and then Herb's mother died of cancer two weeks later. I was also overwhelmed by the fact that I had children. It was different when I only had one child to care for, but now I had two, and I wasn't sure of myself as a mother. For some reason, I was afraid that I was going to overfeed Corey, burp him too hard, sleep through his crying, and totally forget about Marques. I believed if I lost some of the weight I'd gained with Corey's pregnancy, I would feel better about myself and get out of the slump I had fallen into. Before starting my diet and exercise routine, though, I needed an extra boost of will power to motivate me. I heard that reading the Bible could help people do anything so I decided I would read the Bible, starting with Genesis and going all the way to the end of Revelation's to see what would happen.

By the time I got through the middle of Isaiah, something about me was different. I stopped cursing and started praying every morning and night. My heart would leap for joy and skipped beats as I read through the scriptures. The same comfort of love I felt with God at age thirteen was present within me then, too. It was an indescribable feeling, but I knew it had to be real and have some significance in my life.

Once again, I wasn't sure what was occurring within me. But, I became so intrigued with the Bible, learning all the new information about God and the salvation He granted that my preoccupation with losing weight wasn't my main focus anymore. Memorizing scriptures and trying to understand what I read took precedent.

I had tons of questions about what I was supposed to do with God after I read through the entire Bible in three months. *Was I created in God's image? And if so, what did that mean? Did God have a mission and purpose for me like he had for Abraham, Moses, Deborah, Ruth, or Esther?* How was I supposed to know what my purpose was? I longed for answers, but I was ashamed and too embarrassed to bring the subject up with the people that I hung around. I didn't want my family or friends to think that I had turned religious or churchy or have them tease me about being a Holy Roller, running around the church screaming hallelujah and saying that I was a hypocrite. So, I kept my interest about God a secret, just like I had done when I was thirteen.

Eventually though, I returned to Missionary Baptist Church where Herb and I were married at two years ago. I believed being around church people to search out my thousands of questions and to get answers was safe. For some reason, I had a preconceived notion that all people who attended church knew God and what their purpose was.

During that time I actually lost a few pounds and was slowly accepting the deaths of my friend and mother-in-law. Marques and Corey kept me busy and were a joy to have around. Herb was working full-time by then at the Post Office and moonlighting at Carol Publishing Company in Secaucus. His sixty-thousand dollar yearly salary, and my unemployment checks, allowed me to stay home from work for eight months with Corey. I had been a sales representative selling life insurance and wasn't sure if I wanted to continue in that line of work. These were blessings I was learning to be thankful for. I started thanking God for my food, the clothes on my back, my house and everything in it. I would even talk out loud to God and shout praises in the name of Jesus. Corey would look up at me like I was crazy and smile. I smiled, too, thinking that if Herb or any of our friends saw me, they would really commit me to the loony bin.

As time went on, God became my best friend, and I talked to the Holy Spirit about everything. I still hid my closeness and love for God from everybody, including Herb. I wasn't sure what he would say or think of me, but it was becoming more and more difficult to hide it. We entertained a lot during the summer months at our home and went out to different social events when Herb could get the time off from work. Surprisingly, I realized that the conversations that once interest me bored me to tears. I'd rather been at home on my couch curled up reading the Bible. Also, watching Herb drinking himself to death from the green bottles of Heineken turned me off even more.

Herb knew that I loved to read so one day I just left my red Bible sitting on the coffee table. When he walked passed and asked who was reading the Bible, I was nervous, but told him I was. He asked why and I said because I like the stories and enjoyed learning about God. Half jokingly, I told him he should read the Bible, too. He just kept walking into the kitchen without answering me.

I prayed most times in my bedroom, kneeling down on my knees, or in the car. I talked to God about the amount of drinking Herb was doing. I was afraid he was an alcoholic. There were as many green bottles in the refrigerator as there were baby bottles. I had to slide them out of the way in order to reach a baby bottle. Herb and I joked about that, but I knew it wasn't funny when he was no longer bringing home a six pack, but a whole case.

When he was sober, I tried as gingerly as possible to talk to him about his drinking. His answer was always the same—he could stop anytime and for me not to worry. But, when friends and relatives started bringing him home from the Post Office in the early hours of the morning, drunk out of his skull and puking his brains out, I worried all the more. There were no more excuses I could tell myself. I could no longer deny what Herb was, even if he and his family did. He was an alcoholic at age twenty-eight and probably earlier than that. Believing it was my duty to change or fix him, I kept the house cleaned, cooked dinner every day, washed clothes, took care of Marques and Corey, made love to him, and tried not to argue with him when I believed he was wrong. None of what I did stopped him from drinking. In fact, things only grew worse.

Marques and Corey came to church with me every Sunday. Recovering from a drinking binge the night before, Herb was asleep most times on the brown leather recliner that sat between the living room and dining room. Each week was worse than the week before. I was too embarrassed to ask the people in the church to pray for him. Besides being embarrassed, I was also fearful that they would talk about me and think that I was somehow the cause of his drinking problem.

Most of the members had family that had been a part of the church for years and were raised in the Baptist tradition, including Herb's family. (His mother and sister Bertha were long-time members.) For that reason, I felt like an outsider, even though I became an active member in the Inspirational Choir, Sunday school, and assisted wherever I was needed, especially when Women's Day rolled around or the Pastor's anniversary. Also, I loved and trusted in God and was faithful in my commitment to attend church services every Sunday with my children.

At the end of 1989, I decided to go back to work to keep from thinking so much about my problems. I was working in the operations department of a bank at Harborside in downtown Jersey City. I photo copied checks of businesses accounts and keyed the amounts into the computer. But by the middle of 1990, Herby was not only drinking, he started gambling, too. The mortgage and car insurance were being paid, and I had my own money so I didn't question what I believed to be a casual betting habit on sports—besides he was winning. I also reassured myself that Herb was smart and could handle money and wouldn't do anything stupid to jeopardize our financial stability.

In my mind, I hoped things would work themselves out. I had no clue how to fix Herby and stop him from drinking or gambling, and eventually from using cocaine, in the same way that I couldn't stop him from calling me a bitch or stupid ass. I ignored the gnawing in the pit of my stomach and trusted Herb with our lives, thinking because he was the man, he knew something that I didn't. To the outside world, we appeared to be the young perfect couple who was so much in love and did everything together. That's the image we continued to present.

Before we got married, as well as early in the marriage, yelling and cursing at each other were our forms of communication when Herb was drunk. We would argue, and sometimes Herb would stand in the middle of the living room floor in our apartment and growl at me with veins popping out of his neck. In the heat of the argument, he would call me a bitch or tell me to suck out of his ass. He always ended his tirade with "Bitch, I'll kill you if you keep fucking with me!" Then, I would put my hands on my size 14 hips and scream at the top of my lungs for him to kiss my black ass and go fuck himself!

From my childhood, this type of behavior seemed so normal that the words would roll right off me. Back then, it was easy for me to explain away our actions. We were young and didn't mean what we said. We made up with a good night of hot passionate sloppy kisses and a hundred I'm sorry's in between. As we got older and had two young children to raise, I grew tired of the name-calling and the chaos his drinking caused.

After reading the Bible, I stopped going word for word with Herby. All the sex, flowers, and I'm sorry's no longer covered up the words that were cutting into my spirit that Herb spewed at me. No matter how shamefully he hauled his vulgar attacks at me I would not give him the satisfaction of a response.

Unfortunately, this would anger him more, causing the slaughter of words to last longer. Sometimes I would sit on the edge of the bed crying, begging him to stop, but he was so full of rage, that a glassy haze would appear in his eyes, making him seem so far away.

The more chaotic our relationship became, the more I read my Bible and turned to God. The scripture in Proverbs 2:1-6 in the New International Bible that spoke of guidance, wisdom, understanding, knowledge, and insight for my life was a big help and comfort for me. But, early in 1994, I lost focus and control of my temper and attacked Herby physically. We were in our bedroom, and he was getting dressed to go out somewhere. He was standing by the bed, and I was sitting on it, telling him that he needed to spend more time with our children and that they missed him. That started an argument, and the next thing I knew, he quickly swirled around and said, "You are nothing but a stupid ass-nagging bitch! Suck out of my ass and die!"

Before I could catch myself, I leapt off the bed and gave him a hard push. He fell back onto the bed, and I jumped on top of him and began punching him in the chest, screaming with each hit that, "I'm not a bitch! I'm not a bitch! Stop calling me that!"

He flipped me over onto my back after I stopped swinging and sat on me. Tears were pouring from my eyes, and he kept saying how sorry he was. After that, I held even tighter to the scripture in Proverbs and others; praying to God constantly for understanding of my life and marriage. I asked myself over and over, why did Herb and I treat each other that way? Why wasn't Herb as tired of the craziness as I was? I knew that there had to be an answer, and I prayed to find one.

I mentioned to no one how miserable I was, not even my best friend Sharon. She had moved to Alabama with her daughter in September of 1990 to start a new life of her own. I didn't want to burden her with my problems, especially when I wasn't sure what exactly the problem was. Herb's drinking too much and cursing me out was normal for Sharon too. She could string words together in the blink of an eye and royally bless someone out.

Herb, Sharon, my other friends and I all grew up seeing relationships like the one I was experiencing. I just didn't know how deep the words and other violent behaviors penetrated the depths of the other women's spirits. No one openly spoke about his or her emotional suffering. And, I wasn't about to be the first. Why complain? Herb was a good provider and worked hard. He was educated, well liked and didn't bother anybody (except me). Most times, I felt lucky to have him, especially after becoming pregnant with Marques.

I still felt lucky that he stayed by me. I was only nineteen when I gave birth to Marques in February of 1982. I had no job, no skills and only a high school diploma. I left Morgan State University at the end of my freshman year and Herb graduated from Glassboro State College a year later. By the time Marques was two, we had moved into an apartment together, and I was enrolled in Jersey City State College, feeling luckier than ever.

Along with that, I gave up track, which was a great love for me. I believed that once I had a baby, my needs no longer existed. If there was a man in my life, I thought, I was supposed to provide for his and the baby's needs first.

After a year of being on welfare, I found a job at a factory tagging clothes for Gimbles. I was bringing home one hundred and twenty-five dollars a week. Herb was working at Lyle Stuart's, (which later became Carol Publishing Communications) making three hundred dollars. We both worked full time during the day, and I went to school full time in the evenings. Herb watched Marques while I attended college and helped me study and write my papers. Sometimes, he just wrote them himself. Most women I knew were not so lucky.

We were together for six years before we got married. Marques was four-years-old and the ring bearer in our wedding. He looked so cute in his white tuxedo and light-blue cummerbund. I was so proud that I was able to marry the man who had fathered my child and defy all the statistics that stated we wouldn't stay together.

As lucky as I sometimes felt, though, life was not easy with three children and an alcoholic husband. But having a man in my life was the important thing, and I had to do whatever it took to keep him there. He was my man and in trouble. It was my duty as a woman and wife to take care of him and make him feel like a man (at least that's what society taught me). *If only I knew how to do that.* My whole existence and identity was depending upon it. *Who would I be without him?* With God's help, I figured if I could somehow get him to stop drinking, then he wouldn't call me all those ugly names or gamble and use drugs.

The drinking didn't stop; the gambling got worse; and, I wasn't sure how often he used cocaine. Emotionally, I was beaten down. I was depressed all the time. There were days that I didn't get out of the bed to go to work or take care of my children. Herb would take Marques to school and Corey to the babysitter. He would lean over the bed with such concern in his eyes and tell me how much he loved and needed me. I would just cry. Those words were like a big slap in the face. Our lives were falling apart, and he was talking about love and need as if that could fix the problem.

I felt trapped and stuck in a life that I had no desire to be a part of anymore. I believed in the phrase that said, "You made your bed, now lie in it." So, I never considered leaving during that time. To compensate for my misery though, I shopped and spent money that we didn't have, on clothes and shoes for me, trying to fill the numerous voids within me. I had so many shoes by the time Herb had his accident at the end of 1991 that I had to give some away. But for short periods of time, I felt better.

I sprung into action though when Herby was laid up in the Jersey City Medical Center. He had totaled my 1989 Bonneville and depleted our finances. People from the Post Office and Carol Communications took up collections, adding up to about twenty-five hundred dollars. I used that money to pay up the past due mortgage of two months and the car insurance. I bought a 1978 blue and white Cadillac Fleetwood from an auction with my mother's help, and used Herby's sick pay and my checks to put some money in the bank and pay the rest of the bills.

My two children and I moved in with my mother for awhile. It was easier getting back and forth to work and the hospital. I worked in Jersey City. The hospital was in Jersey City. Marques and Corey's school and babysitter were in Jersey City. The only thing we did in Irvington was sleep. (It was less expensive buying property in Essex County than it was in Hudson County.) Even the church that I attended was in Jersey City.

For the first time in a long time I was in total control of my own life. Even though I had to fix all of what Herb messed up and deal with his family not speaking to me, I was at peace. My mother noticed the calm that was over me and some of the friends I had made at church commented on how good I looked. I welcomed the relief but felt somewhat guilty, knowing that the doctors only gave Herb a fifty-percent chance of surviving.

I was twenty-nine, three months pregnant, and did not want to be a widow. Marques was nine and Corey was two. I prayed feverishly for Herb's life, begging God to give him another chance so we all would have an opportunity for a different and better life.

17

Acceptance

A week after I was released from University Hospital, and three days after Herb's funeral, my mother and I had to go back to the house in Irvington to get my marriage license. I needed the certificate to prove to the people at various banks that I was Herb's wife in order to withdraw the money he had in his accounts. (Herb had several accounts without my name on them and the marriage license was the only legal document that they would accept.)

My crutches were under my arms, and my mother was standing to the side of me as we climbed step by step up to the gray wooden porch and stood in front of the white, screened door. I was terrified but too afraid to let my mother know. I wanted to turn and run rather than face what was on the other side of the door. But, I was Vonny; the one everybody thought was so strong she could withstand anything. So, I put the key into the lock and turned, pushing the door slightly open with my trembling hand. The gush of death came rushing out at me, taking my breath away. I stiffened and held tight to my crutches; afraid the force would knock me over. I don't know if my mother saw me or felt what I felt. I was too embarrassed to look at her in case what I felt blow in my face was really just my imagination. She would see my stricken eyes and wonder what the heck was wrong with me. Then, I would have to explain to her what just happened if she asked. (*What would I say? "Oh, Mommy, death met me at the door and tried to claim my life again."*) So, I pretended that I was the brave Vonny that everybody wanted me to be (including me), and moved through the door as if it was a normal, every day occurrence, like brushing my teeth or coming home after work.

I wish that I could go back in time to that day and walk back up onto the porch. If I could, I would scream out, "I can't do this! I can't do this!" I would yell for my mother to take me away and not care about trying to be strong or normal. There was nothing normal about spirits of death flying in my face or going back to a house in which I was almost killed a week and a half before. *Why do I have to pretend that it is?* I don't know if I thought I was pretending at the time. I prayed to God to give me the strength to do what needed to be done. There was no one else to do it; at least, no one offered to help. So, with my faith and trust in God, I did what I did best and that was numb my emotions to the pain in order to take care of business.

No one knew where the marriage license was except for me. Even Herb didn't know where I'd left it. I had no other choice but to go back to that house, in spite of the fact that I wanted to scream at the young black woman behind the desk at one bank and the busy white man at the other bank, "Please don't make me go back, I was almost killed there!" How silly I would have looked.

I was drained. Empty. Depleted. The events of the past few weeks had taken their toll on me, and I couldn't find my way back to God's arms—He seemed so far away. Emotionally, I had no more to give and was afraid I couldn't hold it together anymore. I was scared—but more so for my children. Their daddy had already left them and now, I too, wished to check out. I dreamed of going to a place where no one could expect anything from me. I prayed to go where I didn't have to be responsible for myself or anyone else for that matter. Going insane seemed like the logical choice. Rev was right—going crazy was a choice, and I was making it. I would never commit suicide like Herb did, but going insane was like being dead. I would just die a slower death in a mental hospital somewhere, willing myself to die. It just seemed easier to lose myself in insanity than to accept the realities before me, especially all the false images of my life and marriage with Herb.

When Herb came in the delivery room with me when Corey was born, that was real, right? His presence was so loving and caring. There was nothing abusive or controlling about that—right? Or when he helped plan my baby

198

shower.

I gave birth to Corey on an early Saturday morning at the end of February in 1989—the day that my family, friends, and Herb had planned a surprise baby shower for me. After the delivery, I was rolled back to my room, and Herb kept leaving and returning. Eventually, in a weak voice, I asked him what was he doing. He convinced me he was making phone calls to let everyone know that I had the baby and was all right. (Corey wasn't due until March.) I told him that was so sweet and kissed him on the lips. *How wonderfully blessed I am to have a man like him and a good daddy for my children.* Later, I learned that Herb was really canceling the plans for the baby shower that day and making new ones for the next Saturday with my family and friends. I loved him even more the next week when I found out the true story. *There aren't many men who would get involved with such womanish things like baby showers, and go through great lengths to keep it a surprise, but mine does.*

Then, there was the time in December of 1989 when he gave me the twenty-five hundred dollars for the down payment on my new Bonneville. He also gave me the beautiful brown leather coat for Christmas that same year and the long black leather coat the next Christmas, and, oh yeah, the gorgeous fur coat in 1994. There were also the gold rope chains; the thick herringbone necklace and gold bangles; the gold watches for birthday presents and anniversary gifts; and the seven-day cruise to Bermuda in 1994 for a Valentine's Day gift. Also, what about the small surprise birthday celebration for my twenty-second birthday in 1984; the beautiful gold diamond nugget engagement ring in 1985 for my Christmas present; and the half carat diamond ring in August of 1986 on our wedding day?

That was all real—right?

Then again, stumbling through my house on crutches was real; and so was seeing the spots of blood in the dining room on the carpet where Herby shot himself; and so is the bullet that is still lodged in my head and foot and the one that the doctor removed from my thigh a week later when he extracted the thirty-three staples from my stomach with a staple-puller. Herby gave me all that, too, along with the 10-inch scar below my ribs. Also, don't forget all the emotional scars on my heart that intersect like major thoroughfares after being called a bitch, a slut, a whore, and a stupid ass for so many years.

July 4, 1988 was real, too. I was two and half months pregnant with Corey when we were at a cookout at his sister Bertha's house, and Herby was drunk three times over. I, of course, had earned an unofficial master's degree from Herb's drunken stupors. I knew how to keep myself out of his line of fire. Somehow, near the end of the cookout, I allowed myself to get drawn into a confrontation with him. By the time I realized what was happening, it was too late.

"You Stupid Ass Bitch!" he fired off. "I don't know why the fuck I married you! You get on my Goddamn nerves!"

His eyes were glassy, and his speech was slightly slurred, but he was loud and said all this in front of our six-year-old son Marques, and our friends, Kevin and Candie, and *his* whole family.

Stung. That's what I remember feeling, stung. Stung by fifty million bees with venom more poisonous than a rattlesnake. Somehow or other, my feet began moving me toward the basement door. In the background of my static brain, I heard Bertha say, "What did she do now?"

What did I do? That's what I would like to know!

Bertha's words, coming right after Herby's attack, kept stinging me the entire ten blocks that I walked home. I didn't know who I hated most—Bertha, Herb, or myself. I thought of the song I used to sing as a child to shield me from cruel attacks, "Sticks and stones may break my bones, but words will never hurt me." In reality, those vicious words were hurting real bad—bad enough to know that at age twenty-six I was in big trouble. Exactly what kind of trouble, I wasn't sure yet. I didn't even know there was a name for it then.

To help me cope, I quickly rationalized that it was all my fault. *If Herby wasn't drinking and I didn't allow myself to get drawn into his stupid-ness, then that would have never happened.* Each time after that when Herby would call me a stupid ass bitch or a slut or whore, I would make myself remember that it was my fault for the next time, and the next time, and the next time. Each time I would pick myself up and move on with my life.

Facing the reality of almost being killed by husband wouldn't allow me to pick myself up and move on with my life. I just couldn't shake myself free from the ugly darkness of despair after the shooting. It hung over me like a thunderous rain cloud. Everywhere I went the doom and gloom followed. *How did my life become so meaningless? What did I do to deserve sixteen years of hell? Weren't there any good times? When did everything go wrong?*

Maybe to try to answer my own questions—or maybe just to escape my unhappiness—I kept thinking about when Herby and I first started dating in 1980. I was voted the number one All-County sprinter in Hudson County for the 100 and 200 meters and set a new meet record in Kearny, New Jersey, in the 100 meters of 11.1. I was also accepted at Morgan State University in Baltimore, Maryland. At eighteen, I felt very confident about who I was, especially how I carried myself as a young lady and the fashionable way I dressed.

I was one hundred and twenty pounds and a perfect size 10. I had a pretty face and a slightly long, skinny neck. My breast was a modest 32B that accentuated my slim twenty-seven inch waistline. My behind curved at just the right angle above my tight, muscular thighs and shapely, thick calves.

Herb was going into his third year of college at Glassboro State College in South Jersey, New Jersey and, above all, appeared secure and confident, too. He was very attentive, affectionate and thoughtful of my needs. He took me places that I needed to go, like to the mall, Path Mark, and the beauty parlor. He also would hold my hand, open doors for me, tell me how much he loved me and say how lucky he was that I was his woman. So, when he was adamantly opposed to me wearing stretch pants and semi low-cut tops, I, without many questions, gave in—in spite of the fact that I didn't feel comfortable being told what I could wear. I figured that I would change him later. When he expressed so much jealousy about all the male friends I had and insisted that I stop seeing them, I did. I reasoned, *oh, he really loves me and he wants me all to himself. So, what is the problem?*

Debra, the domestic violence advocate for Orange County, told me soon after I had left home that that kind of behavior was about power and control. *How was I supposed to know that? It wasn't in a textbook anywhere. And if it were, what would I have done?* At age thirty-four I was still trying to make the connection. The dots were not fusing together in my head. They were presenting a picture of my life that was unrecognizable. *Was my life really like all those other battered women?*

I yearned to close my eyes and drown out all the voices and images by weaving a web in my head. But, the faces of all the white women, African-American women, and Latino women that I had seen in the domestic violence support groups kept peeking in and out of the silky threads. The horrific stories they shared of being beaten, kicked, punched, stabbed, spit on, choked, thrown from one end of a room to the next, played charades with my own reality.

I remember sitting in that cold, pictureless room at the YMCA. My children played happily in that room just a few months before I returned to go through the screening process. If the walls could only speak, they held the silence of the pain of secrets to each woman's heart that dared to bleed truth to her existence. I looked around the room at the faces of the women trying to find some commonality with them. We were all women, yes, but I was not one of them. I was having a really difficult time accepting the definition that roped me in as an abused woman and Herby as a batterer.

He never stabbed me in my leg with a pair of scissors because I didn't move fast enough when he called me—like one husband did. Phones weren't being snatched out of walls while I was speaking. I was never forced to have sex with him, or made to stay up all night. I wasn't walking around on eggshells afraid anything that I did would set him off.

When I relayed to the group that Herb would call me a bitch or an asshole, I still didn't feel abused, mainly because I would get back at him by not washing his clothes, not cooking dinner for him, or not having sex with him. If he'd ever hit me, we would have been in for a long night because I could fight. Then, there would be a bigger mess once my family got involved.

Debra, who was also the facilitator of the Newburgh support group, then asked me why did I leave my husband and go into a shelter.

"Because he threatened to kill me. But I don't believe he will really do that. He's threatened me so many times in the past and nothing happened. I won't go back because we have so many other problems with his gambling habit, messing up money and not respecting me as a woman and person."

She explained to me that name-calling and making threats against someone's life was verbal and emotional abuse that could potentially lead to violence. But at the time, I couldn't understand how that was possible. I told her people were called names everyday and not hurt. Besides, Herby wasn't a physically violent person. That just wasn't his nature.

To be honest, now that I look back on our lives together, I don't really know what Herby's true nature was. I was so dependent upon God during those chaotic times that I believed He would protect me before anything violent happened. Unaware of how much danger I was really in, I eventually stopped going to the Newburgh support group and started my own in May of 1996, more in the hope of sharing common spiritual principals with other women than protecting myself from Herby.

The support group was held on Wednesday nights at 7:00 p.m. in my apartment on Grand Street. There were four other women beside myself that attended—Laura, Annie, Mary, and Martha. We had all met through Reverend Lewis, either from the church he started in February of that same year or from the workshops he facilitated once a week in Newburgh.

In the support group each week, we discussed issues that were affecting our lives in a positive or negative way and how they related to our spiritual journey and understanding of God. I shared the stories of the women from the Newburgh support group and was open and honest with Laura, Annie, Mary, and Martha about my denial of believing that Herby could possibly hurt me physically and the detachment I felt from the other women at the Newburgh support group.

Laura, who was also separated from her husband due to abuse, alcohol, and drugs was the first to say that Herb's behavior was unpredictable and suggested that I work on acceptance and hold to my trust and faith in God. The spiritual connection that I experienced with those women every Wednesday evening soon offered what seemed to me a more realistic view of my life. The group continued to meet until the shooting.

Days passed after returning to the house in Irvington as I looked back on my life, and still there was no change in my mental condition. I could sit in the midst of my family and laugh and engage in conversation and no one knew I was going crazy. *Is this what it was like for Herb? Was he mentally ill and slowly went insane? Could it really have been that Herb was just controlling and I didn't go along with his program? Did I deserve to be almost killed?*

Those questions plagued me along with the nightmares that started after I was released from the hospital. They grew worse and became more frequent as my stress level increased. I never mentioned the dreams to my family or anyone during that times. I figured they were only dreams and couldn't hurt me, so what was the point. But, they did hurt.

In the dreams, Herby came back to life and found me no matter where I was or who I was with. He chased me through woods, tunnels, and houses with a .22 caliber black gun saying, "I just gotta put one more bullet in her head." I always jolted awake, out of breath, barely escaping. When the nightmare ended, I spent the whole day looking over my shoulder, thinking that Herb was coming back to kill me.

As time went on, the reality of my past and present life slowly began to set in. The most disheartening and hurtful truth I had to admit to myself was the fact that my husband's dying was the best thing that could have happened, given the situation. Had Herb still shot me and lived, he would be in jail and my children and I would have nothing. We would have lost everything. Because of Herby's death, the four of us are able to live. The guilt I felt over wanting to go insane, knowing that God spared my life, and so many people telling me what a miracle I was ate me up inside. I thought about the phrase that I'd heard in church: "God don't put no more on us than we can bear."

But I was falling.

I will lift up mine eyes unto the hills,
form whence cometh my help.
My help cometh from the Lord,
which made heaven and earth.
He will not suffer thy foot to be moved:
he that keepeth Israel shall neither slumber nor sleep.
The Lord is thy keeper:
the Lord is thy shade upon thy right hand.
The sun shall not smite thee by day,
nor the moon by night.
The Lord shall preserve thee from all evil:
he shall preserve thy soul.
The Lord shall preserve thy going out
and thy coming in
from this time forth,
and even for evermore.
Psalm 121

18

Rebellion

I want to know why girls always have to do all of the housework; while, boys only take out the garbage and mop the floor (and they half do that). I'm never going to do all this housework by myself when I grow up and get married I told myself over and over while standing at the ironing board in my bedroom, ironing twenty million white blouses. But, I never said a word out loud.

There were eight of us by then—six girls and two boys. I was the oldest girl. We all went to Catholic school, except for Fatima, who was the baby. We had to wear white blouses and blue skirts, and the boys wore white shirts with blue pants. That was the uniform code at St. Bridget's.

Mommy made me iron all the blouses for my four sisters and me. We each had five blouses apiece. The green round plastic laundry basket was filled with nothing but white, short sleeve blouses. *Why dey can't iron their own stupid blouses? Why Mommy can't iron dem, dey her kids not mine?* I would say this in my head every time I had to iron those blouses—relieved that Mommy could not read my thoughts.

She would call, "Vonny, get the basket and start ironing."

"Ugh!" She didn't have to say iron what; I already knew.

The creepy, crawly headache would set in. All the ugly thoughts of being a girl, and the oldest girl at that, would bunch up together in my head and almost cause me to have a heart attack. At least, that's what I wished would happen. But, I had no such luck. I would drag my weak knobby knees and buffalo head down the dimly lit hallway of our apartment to my bedroom where the white, monstrous chore awaited me.

Flicker! Flicker! Flicker! my fingers went as I sprinkled the cold water from the cup onto the wrinkles of the blouses. (We couldn't afford spray starch so the tap water would have to do.) Sizz! This is what the sound of the steam made from the iron if I plopped too much water in one place on the blouses instead of flicking the water out across them. I would have to hold the iron down longer in order to dry up the wet spot. Thus, I made sure that I was careful to flicker and not plop so I could hurry up and finish and go outside.

After ironing the blouses, I had to hang them separately on the copper wire hangers—buttoning the top button so they wouldn't slide off and fall to the floor and become dirty or wrinkled again. I then would have to figure out whose white blouse was whose because they were all almost the same size and looked exactly alike. (Tonja was two years younger than I; Jeanette was a year younger than Tonja; Yvette was a year younger than Jeanette; and Andrea was three years younger than Yvette.) I then had to place them in each sister's closet, not caring who got whose blouse, as long as I got all of mine.

Didn't I prove to Mommy that it couldn't be true that girls were only good at housework and boys were good at everything else? I rushed home from school one day to tell her that I had beaten all but one boy in track from the seventh and eight grades, including my brother William. I was so proud of myself and needed my mother to be equally proud of me and stop making a difference between my brother and me just because I was a girl.

Mommy knew I was just as good at playing tops as my brother William. I sat on the ground, spread my legs like the boys, and dug into the blacktop with a sharp stick, bringing up enough tar to mash down in my top so that it would have enough weight to glide over the concrete ground where the square top boxes were. I had also mastered the art of spinning a top and scooping it up between my fingers into the middle of my hand while it was still spinning.

She also knew that her thirteen-year-old daughter would challenge any myth that said, "A girl couldn't do or wasn't supposed to do," and still know how to act like a lady. However, there I was stuck in the house because I was girl, slaving over the ironing board singing, "plop-plop, fizz-fizz, oh what a relief it is" and falling out on my bed from sheer mental exhaustion after finishing the last blouse. Still she never listened—or I just never told her how I felt.

And after all these years I was still trying to prove myself—only this time it was with my husband. I just didn't know where I fit. Herby wanted the traditional lifestyle of a marriage where the husband went to work and came home to a clean house and dinner on the table, even though I had to work outside of the home and still take care of the children. I felt whoever got home first should cook dinner and do whatever needed to be done around the house. We all lived there, and we were a family so what difference did it make who did what? This was a constant argument between us. He didn't understand why I couldn't happily accept my role as a wife and mother like all the other women he knew. My response to him was always the same.

"Just because I'm a woman, don't mean I have to do all the cooking, cleaning, and disciplining the children. Slavery is over, and I work just like you do. I bet some man came up with that idea to suit his own needs, and I don't have to like it."

Throughout the marriage though, I ended up doing most of the cooking, cleaning, and taking care of the kids anyway, continuously struggling to keep the peace by fitting into that box or set of rules that were already defined for me as a woman without my permission.

When Herb began to slowly control the money in 1993, I no longer cared about all the things he bought me, keeping the peace, or walking around with my head stuck in the sand like an ostrich, pretending that everything was all right. It all started when Herby was in the hospital for six months after his car accident and one of the nurses that was attending to him notified me that he was eligible to qualify for Social Security Benefits due to all his major injuries. So, I called the Social Security office to check into the information, and they mailed me a ten-page application with about one hundred questions to be filled out by the doctors and Herb.

The Federal Government required answers for the kind of injuries he had, how long he would be in the hospital, his educational level, the type of work he did, how much money he made, etcetera... It took about two weeks to answer all the questions, check them over, gather all the documentation of birth certificates, social security cards, and several trips to my local Social Security office in Irvington before I could mail off the application.

After Herb was denied benefits for the third time in the screening process, we were then within our rights to contact a lawyer to fight on our behalf. By then, six months had gone by, and Herb had already been released from the hospital. But, he was in physical therapy as an outpatient and not back at work yet. My three hundred dollar weekly salary and the small amount of money we received from our car insurance disability claim every two weeks was the only source of income. Against Herb's wishes and pride, I applied for food stamps in order that we would have food on the table. Both of us were devastated when we received the last letter stating that the Social Security doctors felt in spite of all the injuries Herb sustained, including the loss of an eye, that he was young and had a good education, so therefore, he should be able to do something.

"Something. He should be able to do something." The phrase just kept ringing over and over in my head while sitting at the dining room table with my husband and a blank look on my face with neither one of us saying anything. *Were they crazy! 'Doing something' wasn't going to pay the bills!* The letter slowly dropped from Herb's hands onto the table. He stared at me with tears in his eyes as if he were reading my mind and burst out crying uncontrollably. I rushed to my husband's side, standing over him, I gently pulled his head to my breast saying, "Babe, please don't cry. It'll be all right. I'll take care of everything. We'll go to the lawyer and fight this. It's gonna be okay."

A year later after Herb returned to work part-time at both jobs, a Judge ruled favorably in our court case. He awarded Herby retroactive money in one lump sum, tax free, going back to the time of the accident in 1991. On top of that, Herb received twenty-two hundred dollars a month for himself, and one hundred and forty-four dollars a month for each of our three children, and for me until his doctors gave him a clean bill of health to return to work full-time.

That time while sitting at the dining room table reading the letter, we both had the biggest smiles on our faces that I ever remember seeing. We joyfully embraced each other, and Herby thanked me for sticking by him and fighting for our family and keeping my faith in God. While our excitement was still pretty high, I jokingly sang out, "I get a big one hundred and forty-four dollars."

"No you don't!" Herb said too seriously. "This is *my* money!"

"Oh, get outta here, Herb. Stop playing," I said with laughter still in my voice and a flimsy wave of my hand. "This is *our* money!"

"I'm not playing, Lavon! You're not touching this money! It's mine!"

My stomach dropped to my knees, my heart pounced down to where my belly was supposed to be, and I forgot to breathe, almost passing out from shock. I quickly scanned through my brain to come up with something reasonable to say in order to restore the moment of joy we had just experienced as a couple.

"Herby, we are a family," I said through clinched teeth and pleading, tearful eyes. "The money that comes into the house by you or me is not *yours* or *mine; it's ours.* I fought with Social Security because I love you and did everything I did for us as a family—not just for you. You didn't even know you qualified for Social Security until I told you in the hospital."

"So what do you want, a pat on the back? If I didn't bust my ass working all the time, you wouldn't had anything to fight for!"

"But Herb, I help you work the way you do. I take care of the kids and the house so you don't have that added responsibility and burden. We work together as a family."

"Well, I'm the one who had the accident so it's *my* money, and I can do what I want with it."

"But... You know what Herb, you're right. How stupid of me to think any different."

I slowly got up from the table feeling spit on, squashed like a gnat, and rejected. I walked up the stairs to my bedroom with my heart between my legs, leaving Herb at the table with his letter of joy—not giving my crushed spirit a second thought. I lay down on the bed and cried tears of blood, wailing out to God for comfort and begging Him to take me out of my misery. *Who was that man downstairs impersonating my husband? God, please shield me from another storm.*

I constantly prayed, asking God to please send someone into my life that would have my best interests at heart and help me find my spiritual purpose. The life that I had shared with Herby for fourteen years at that point was at a dead end. I think it was during that time I subconsciously withdrew totally from Herby emotionally and knew for sure that I was on my own, in spite of the fact that I was married. For the reminder of the two years that we were together after that, I gave little or no affection to him. I couldn't find my heart.

One day in 1994 while I was at home with my three children, I came up with an idea how to make money for the summer. I was working as a substitute teacher then and received no pay during the months of July and August. Herb would take the Jeep leaving the children and me at home without transportation or money. (I very seldom asked him for money anymore after the Social Security incident.) I called my mother to tell her about my great scheme to sell candy outside her building and asked if she would loan me the money to buy the supplies from BJ's in Jersey City. Of course she said yes and asked why did I want to sell candy. I gave her a flimsy excuse about being bored and the children needing to be around their family. I could never tell her that the real reason I needed money was because I would probably have to literally fight Herby for *his* money. (She would have fought him herself or my Uncle Frankie.)

That same day I gathered my children together so we could prepare to take the bus and train to Jersey City. I prayed to God to help me find at least five dollars around the house for bus and train fare. I found two whole dollars and three dollars in change.

Marques and I were the only two I had to pay a fare for. I figured that I could slip Corey through the turnstile and not worry about Sheriah; she was only two and still in the carriage. We made it to Jersey City, no worse for the wear, and my children actually enjoyed riding the bus and train, especially since it was only their second time ever riding on public transportation.

I drove with my mother in her white and blue Dodge 600 SE down to BJ's and brought bulks of lollipops, ring pops, ices, juices, chips, and assorted candy, totaling about thirty dollars. We set the portable aluminum brown table up with all the candy and the cooler filled with ice to keep the juices and ices cold. Before I was ready to sell, the children were coming out of the woodwork waiting to buy the candy and things. I think I made about thirty dollars that day and between ten and fifteen dollars every day after for the entire month of July and parts of August.

The days that I did not make it to Jersey City, my mother or Uncle Frankie sold the candy from her apartment. Additionally, I got the Jeep from Herb after I told him that I needed it to get back and forth with the kids. He was very upset that I was selling the candy, making my own money, and insisted that I stop and stay at home. Each time I ignored him and continued doing my thing. I guess that might be why when all of a sudden he started carrying our two bank books in his black leather bag everywhere he went, I didn't make much of a fuss or care.

The crazier things got between us, the more grateful I became that I had the Lord in my life. There were days when I didn't know if I was coming or going. Herb was no longer drinking, but his behavior was the same. I could not make sense of his rage when he called me an asshole or stupid bitch in front of our children if we got into a disagreement or why he felt the need to hoard all the money, and he was sober!

By 1994, God had undeniably become the light of my life and the only constant joy present in my heart. Sometimes, I was so full of God's word after reading the Bible that I felt drunk. In the midst of all the chaos, I held to my faith and belief that all things were possible, even when I was confused about whether I really wanted to remain married. There was a time though when my prayers were answered and I thought my life with Herby would get better.

During the years of 1993 to 1996, Herb was a recovering alcoholic. He took his recovery seriously and attended the AA meetings faithfully, even if he had to take an hour or two off from work. A few times, I accompanied him for support, but I couldn't identify with the 12 Step concept, or the heavy, thick cigarette smoke that suffocated me so I stopped going.

At the beginning of his recovery, he also started coming to church regularly with the children and me. Every Sunday morning, the five of us would load up in the black Jeep and drive the thirty minutes it took to get to church. He joined the male chorus and participated in Sunday school. On his nights off from the Post Office, we read the Bible together as a family at home and whatever scriptures he didn't understand, I did my best to explain to him. Sometimes, I would call my girlfriend Cynthia if I wasn't sure of the interpretation, and we would have a Bible study over the phone. I encouraged him to read his Bible as often as he could at work and to call me if there was any particular scripture he wished to talk about.

Slowly, we were piecing together a Christian life that I had prayed for, for a long time. Even Marques and Corey seemed happier. (Sheriah was still a baby.) At the end of 1993, Herb was asked to be a "Walking Deacon," along with another Brother of the church. I wasn't sure if he was ready for that big responsibility, especially having just come back into the church after being gone since he was a kid. But, I wanted to be a supportive wife so I prayed to God hoping that this was the right direction for us as a family.

The ceremony took place in November of 1994 at Missionary Baptist Church. Besides the regular members, the church was full of family and friends from front to back and side to side. The choirs sang, and I hired a live contemporary gospel band to perform. Marques and I also worked on a song by the Williams Brothers at home called 'A House Is Not A Home Without God.' He sang the solo acappella and brought the packed church of

214

people to their feet and rivers of tears streaming down Herb's face. The Spirit was moving! I fell in love with my husband all over again and felt the closes that I'd ever felt to God.

Unfortunately, that love was squashed and trampled on within less than a month by Herb's constant out-of-the-blue rage and degrading language directed at me. I cried out to God, asking what was the problem over and over. I didn't know what to do, or how to make my life look like the image in my head of a loving, caring, respectful, happy, Christian couple and family. *Why did my husband treat me as if he hated me? Why couldn't he just love me?*

I became angry with God, withdrawn, and depressed. That left no one's arms for me to run to and feel safe, secure, protected, and loved. I knew couples had their differences and all that, but Herby and I had been beyond differences a long time ago. My children— my poor, poor children, what was I doing to them? How could I have messed their lives up so badly? They had a mother who would fight tooth and nail to protect them from any kind of danger; yet, they were living and experiencing hell in their own home, and I couldn't stop it, even with Jesus being my personal Lord and Savior.

Cynthia was the only person that I finally confided in about the way Herby treated me. We had been friends for over three-years, and I knew that she loved the Lord and that I could trust her not to pass judgment. She was surprised, but supportive. She would always tell me that God had something great planned for me. Usually, I smiled at her or blushed, saying thank you. But a few days before Christmas in 1994, she said those words to me, and I snapped at her saying, "How can God have something great for me when I can't even save my own family?"

On the afternoon of Christmas Eve, I was home by myself and don't remember where my children were, but Herb was at work. I had just finished reading T. D. Jakes' new book, <u>Woman, Thou Art Loose</u>, hoping to regain my faith in God. I lay down on the carpet in the living room and began praying—pounding my fist into the rug and shouting out to God, "What did I ever do to deserve this? Please loose my spirit from the hell I'm living." I continued on like that for about five minutes when all of a sudden I heard this soft, angelic voice as clear as day say, "I love you, and you are going to preach to many people."

I jumped up off the floor and ran into the dining room. I sat down so hard that I cracked the small part of the chair. Sweat was rolling down my face, back, and under my armpits. I closed my eyes and put my head down trying to catch my breath. Visions of Neptune Baptist Church, Missionary Baptist Church, my Uncle Sonny and Aunt Barbara Ann appeared in front of my eyes. Then, I heard the low, sweet voice again say, "By September, your life will be different."

I bolted up from the chair, hitting my left knee on the thick mahogany table leg not sure where to run. So I hopped around in circles trembling before dropping to my knees crying and begging God to take 'IT' away. Lint and dirt from the rug was sticking to my tear-stained face when I got up. I was terrified and really believed that I was losing my mind. I sat back down at the table trying to gather my bearings and make sense of what just happened. My mind could not comprehend so I called Cynthia at home and barely allowed her to say hello, before I breathlessly blurted out what I thought occurred. Once she got me to calm down and to repeat what I said more slowly, everything was quiet for what seemed like a long time after I finished speaking.

"You don't believe me, do you?" I said. "I know it sounds crazy, and I don't know if I believe it myself."

"Oh no, Lavon, I believe you! I was just trying to think of what to say. You've been "called"—chosen by God!"

"No Cynthia, please don't say that. I don't want to be "called" or "chosen." I just want to live a simple, happy, normal life and worship God in the process."

Cynthia's joy was spilling through the phone, but I couldn't rejoice with her. My mind was groggy, and I was still scared out of my wits. We must have talked for two or three hours trying to make sense of the "calling." I loved Cynthia for her enthusiasm, trust in God, and friendship. I only wished that I were as confident as she was in her belief of God choosing me to do something great.

PART FOUR

FACING THE GHOSTS

19

Stop & Go

I left Mommy's house for awhile to think and to get some fresh air. I hopped around the outside of the basketball court with my crutches under my arms on my way to visit Aunt Eleanor, who lived on the other side of the Projects. I desperately wanted to go home, but didn't have a car or good enough credit to finance one. The white Jeep that Herb had had was repossessed. Someone in his family called the finance company posing as me. They informed the people that Herb had passed away and that I didn't want the Jeep. They also gave my mother's name, address, and phone number in case they needed to contact me before taking the Jeep.

When I finally got in touch with the finance company and was told what happened, I was shocked, hurt, and angry; how could people be so cruel and hateful. The woman was very sympathetic to my situation after I explained what my husband did to me and that I never called for them to repossess the Jeep. She tried to work out an arrangement for the kids and I to have the vehicle returned. Unfortunately, the monthly payments were close to six hundred dollars—too expensive for me to manage. What little money I'd retrieved from Herb's bank accounts was enough to help with a down payment, but not sufficient to pay a hefty monthly car note or the twenty-five thousand-dollar debts I had incurred during the marriage.

I also needed to bring some stability to my children's lives, too. They were attending school in Jersey City while we lived with my mother. And I didn't want them to become too attached to their new living environment, especially when I had no intentions of ever moving back to Jersey City or living in the house in Irvington. Marques had already approached me and asked if he could stay with my mother and finish school, but I would not allow him to be separated from me again. We had been in Jersey for three weeks, and I just wanted to get us home to Newburgh so we could begin the long healing process.

On my way to my aunt's house I stopped and spoke to Mutter, Dorothy, Mrs. Rachael and others whose names I don't remember. I had not seen any of them in a long time. They asked if I was all right and gave their condolence for Herb. They also told me how good I looked in spite of what happened to me. I laughed and said, "Thanks." From the way their smiles and concern for me warmed my entire body, I knew they were really glad to see me and happy that I was still alive.

The warmth restored some of the faith in myself that the funeral had crushed earlier in the month. The weather was still pretty mild for the end of September, and the sun was shining brightly. I had on my mother's light-weight green jacket, green nylon sweat pants and a black cotton shirt.

I hobbled along the outskirts of the court, watching the teenage girls huddled in their cliques, the guys banging with each other on the basketball court, the little kids playing kickball and jump rope. I stopped to rest from time to time to stretch my broken leg. The chitter-chatter, noises, people everywhere, and all the going-ons of play brought back a lot of fond memories of my own youthful days growing up in the Project.

By the time I was nine, we had moved from Building 96 to Building 92 because Mommy was expecting her seventh child, and we needed more room. Our new apartment offered four bedrooms instead of the three we had in 96. The living room was the first room you entered when you came into the house. Mommy made us keep that room so spotless that we could eat off the beige, tile floor. We had a floor-model color Zenith television, a new eight-track deck stereo system, a bluish-green paisley couch and love seat with brocade drapes to match, and black African chalk statues of a man and woman hanging on the wall, with an equally exquisite mirror in the center.

There was a long hallway just wide enough for two young kids to walk down side by side that opened off from the living room. About fifteen feet away was a doorway carved out along the left side of the hallway wall, which was the kitchen. We had a large wooden table with six chairs that was in the middle of the floor. That was just enough chairs for my brother, sisters and me, because Troy, who was the baby, sat in his high chair at the corner of the table. There was a yellow washing machine over by the window and close to the sink. The yellow electric dryer was on the other side of the table, against the back wall, next to the other window. The oversized brown and white square freezer sat next to that, taking up three-quarters of the wall space, with the kitchen cabinets and counter top occupying the rest. The refrigerator and stove were kitty-cornered to each other, with the doorway and kitchen closet in the middle of both. The kitchen and living room were always the two busiest rooms in the house, with the bathroom running a close second.

The hallway continued for a few more feet and looped around in a semicircle. A light fixture hanging overhead with a string attached was in the middle of the ceiling. There were four bedrooms and a full size bathroom within the circle. The first bedroom was my sister Tonja's and mine. We shared a large closet that we divided with a colored hanger. I utilized the whole top shelf with all the books I had read. That was Mommy's reward to me for enjoying reading so much. Against the wall, we had two beautiful creamy gloss dressers separated by the old stereo system. On the other wall were our famous high-riser beds that everybody wished they had. We also had the room with the fire escape that people were either always climbing on or banging against.

Mommy and Daddy shared the next room with my baby brother, Troy. They had the traditional oak bedroom suite that came with two matching night stands that were on either side of the bed, an armoire, which I think was Daddy's, and a long dresser with the mirror on top. Their "famous" possession was a baby crib. In the middle of the floor, between the full size bed and long dresser, sat the white crib where Troy slept. That's all I ever remember about Mommy and Daddy's room that never changed, beside the fact they had the biggest room.

In the center was my brother William's room (soon to be shared with Troy). He had a room all to himself for a while because Troy was a baby (lucky break). He had a high-riser bed, too. (Mommy probably discovered she could get a bargain buying two instead of one. She was always searching for bargains and usually found them. Mommy was good at that sort of thing. She had to be.) His bed wasn't as cool as ours because the sheets were always dirty and sloppy. He had two mixed-matched brown dressers with clothes hanging out of them and a closet that clothes never hung from because they were always on the floor. In spite of the smelly foot odor that lingered in his room—taking your breath away—he had the best view from his window of the 'happenings' going-on in the Projects. I spent many days looking out that window when I couldn't go outside due to bad weather or being punished.

Then, there was my three younger sisters' room, Jeanette, Yvette, and Andrea. They had a nice pair of creamy gloss dressers too, along with the largest room of us kids. Their window faced the front of our building. During school days, we had to come upstairs when the first streetlight came on, which was usually around 6:00 p.m. It was still daylight and our friends teased us—calling us early birds as we continued playing with them, hanging out my sisters' window. They could stay out until it got dark—one or two hours later. The girls had a bunk bed in their room. Jeanette slept in the top bunk by herself because she was the older of the two. Yvette and Andrea shared the bottom bed, and all you heard was move over! Watch your feet! You're kicking me!

Then, Mommy yelling from her room, "Y'all be quiet in there and go to sleep!"

The bathroom made up the last of the rooms to complete the semicircle. It was an average size bathroom with a white toilet, sink, and tub. There was no shower—that was a luxury item. I would have given anything to have a shower in our apartment. Since that was the only bathroom for nine people, Mommy developed a system to save time. We took our baths at night so all we had to do in the morning was wipe off and brush our teeth. The three younger girls went together into the bathroom first, then Tonja and next William. Mommy said I took too long, so I went last, which was fine with me because I got to stay in bed and sleep a little longer. Daddy worked at the Dixon Mills Pencil Factory and always left for work before we got up so Mommy didn't have to work him into the system.

A light wind began to blow and the breeze of fresh air felt cool against my skin. By the time I reached the other side of the Projects, I saw more kids jumping rope, playing cards with adults for money and using profanity. Things had sure changed. Besides the jumping rope, none of that would have been tolerated when I was growing up thirty-some-odd years ago. I wouldn't be caught dead saying a curse word in front of an adult, or gambling. I would have been in worse shape than what I was now. In fact, I would have needed more than a car to get me out of town after the adult who heard and saw me spanked my behind and then brought me home to my mother to finish the job!

I remember when I was in kindergarten and Mrs. Hemming, who lived in the Projects, was the teacher's aide in my class. Everyday, the teacher had to tell me to be quiet and stop talking so much. Then one day, Mrs. Hemmingway came up to me real sweet and said, "Lavon, tell your mother I want to see her."

"Okay," I said, with a big smile spreading across my five-year-old face. For the rest of the day I was jittery—couldn't wait to get home to tell Mommy to go see Mrs. Hemming. When I got home, I burst in the house all excited with that same big smile on my face, yelling, "Mommy! Mommy! Mrs. Hemming wants to see you!"

Mommy stopped what she was doing in the kitchen and said, "Okay, I'll be right back."

Mrs. Hemming lived in Building 98—right next to ours. I waited anxiously to hear what good things she had to say about me to my mother. Finally, Mommy returned. She had a strange look on her face. She walked up to me without saying a word and smacked me in my mouth about three times and said, "You better stop that talking in class!"

I stopped to rest my leg again and chuckled to myself as I thought about all the fun I had growing up in the Projects. (In spite of that incident.) There were always plenty of kids to play with my age. If they didn't want to play, I always had my brother, sisters and millions of cousins—Aunt Eleanor had nine children—Aunt Barbara Ann had six, and Mommy had eight. Uncle Frankie's kids were too young, and Uncle Sonny's children were too old and didn't live in the Projects.

We played all kinds of games, johnny-jump-the-white-horse, red-rover, 1-2-3-red-light, hopscotch, tops, kick-the-can, stickball, basketball, seven-minutes-in-heaven, spin-the-bottle... We even created fun with shopping carts from the A&P supermarket that was located behind the Projects. People would bring the shopping carts to the Projects and that would be our joy ride. About four of us would squeeze into the cart while somebody pushed real fast, until they were running. The fun would end after one, or all, of us got hurt and went home crying from either the cart toppling over or crashing into a brick wall.

The leaves on the trees started to rustle from the wind, interrupting my pleasant thoughts. I shook my head and wondered how did my life get from there to here? Being a widow—shot four times—financially broke and secretly wishing that I were either dead or crazy just made no sense to me. Tears formed at the corners of my eyes, falling down on my cheeks. I wiped the tears away with the back of my hand. I had to pull myself together because I could not break down yet. I still had too much to do.

I finally made it to my aunt's house. I was grateful she lived on the first floor, unlike my mother who lived on the top floor. She had a four-bedroom apartment like Mommy use to have. Mommy had moved to a one-bedroom apartment some months earlier because she didn't need all the rooms anymore—it was a rule of the Projects.

My Aunt Eleanor's apartment was smaller and shaped differently. Her dining room was the first room you stepped in, with the kitchenette off to the side. You had to squeeze past the dining room table and chairs to enter the living room. Beyond the living room was a small hallway that the four bedrooms and bathroom surrounded.

Aunt Eleanor was happy to see me and so were my cousins, Deneen, Theresa, and Barbara Jean. They were visiting their mother, too, except for Deneen who still lived at home with her daughter. I had not seen my cousins in almost a year. When they came to the hospital to visit me that was our first time seeing each other again. We sat on the striped grayish couch and talked about old times growing up together and how much it had changed. I was astonished that I didn't know most of the people living there any more. Many of us from my generation had moved out in search for something different, unlike the generations before us. We laughed at the stories we retold about our mothers and ourselves. I gave them details about my separation from Herb and the shooting. We all cried and Aunt Eleanor thanked God that I was still alive and that led to an amiable conversation about God. I spent about two and half-hours there and was ready to journey back to Mommy's house. I had an enjoyable time, my spirits were lifted, and I told my aunt and cousins so. Then, I hugged each of them and said good-bye, hoping to see them before I left.

When I got back outside, the dusk air had grown a little chilly, but it was comfortable. I began the ten-minute walk back that now took me twenty minutes because of the broken foot. Many people were still outside, sitting on the benches enjoying the night air. As I hobbled past, I thought about the many nights I use to sit outside on those same benches during the twenty-one years that I had lived there—and how this is where it all began for me—my initiation into life.

By the time I reached Mommy's building, I had an idea of how to get a car. I needed to speak with my girlfriend Cynthia. I hastened my pace to get upstairs to call her.

Then said Jesus,
Father, forgive them;
for they know not what they do.
And they parted his raiment, and cast lots.
Luke 23:34

20

DÉJÀ VU

After getting off the phone, I was lying on my mother's bed, crying out to God and begging Him to help me. The man from the bank informed me that the mortgage payments were two months behind, soon to be three, and that the insurance company might not pay off the house note because Herb had committed suicide. The bedroom door was closed. I didn't know or care who was in the house that heard me cry. I pounded my fist into the mattress, having a Déjà vu moment, except this one really happened.

Five years earlier I had gone through similar circumstances—back when Herb was in the car accident. I couldn't believe lightening had struck twice in the same place—my heart. I finally emerged from my mother's bedroom, entering the bathroom gloom-stricken. I splashed cold water on my face and swollen red eyes, incapable of shedding another tear. My thoughts were like a labyrinth of the New York City subway. I knelt down on the bathroom floor, laying my head on top of the closed toilet lid, wrapping my arms around the cold porcelain bowl, and asking God to please help me hold on.

Later that day, I told my mother that not only did Herb sign the two-hundred thousand-dollar life insurance policy over to his sister Bertha, and not pay the mortgage, but that the Mortgage Company might not pay off the house because he committed suicide. I could tell from the astounded look on my mother's face as she was reassuring me that it'd be all right, that she wasn't so sure herself. Mommy was the kind of person that did not show much emotion. So, when the expression on her face portrayed so much hurt and anger, I was instantly sorry that I told her. I knew if all my disastrous misfortunes could cause my mother to grimace, I was knee deep in shit. I hated Herb for the hundredth time at that moment. I turned to my mother and said, "Remember when I sold life insurance seven years ago?"

"Yeah," she said.

"Mommy, there's only a two year suicide clause in effect. After the second year of owning the policy, the clause no longer stands, no matter what kind of insurance it is."

"That's right."

"So, Herby and I had that insurance on the house for eight or nine years now. The insurance company has to pay off my house."

"Did you tell the man that?"

"Yeah, but he was so adamant about them not paying because of the suicide, I don't think he was hearing me. I'm gonna call him back tomorrow and tell him again because I don't think that clause has changed in the last seven years. Maybe he doesn't know."

"Right. He may only deal with the mortgage payments and not the insurance part."

"You know what Ma? The insurance company probably will pay off the past due mortgage, too. Remember when Herb totaled my Bonneville in 1991 and I told you the finance people called me at my job telling me I still had to send in my payments until the insurance paid the car off?"

"Yeah."

"Well, I never sent them the money and when the insurance company sent me the check after they paid for my car, they deducted the late payments from my settlement and paid me the difference."

"Make sure you call them tomorrow."

"Yeah, I will. My head doesn't hurt so much anymore. I'm gonna call Rev and talk to him."

I called my pastor that night and told him everything that transpired. He agreed with my plan and encouraged me to remain strong. I admitted to him how hard it was becoming for me to stay strong and sane.

"Vonny, listen to me. I am very proud of you. I know you've had a lot to deal with in the last ten months, but it's going to get better. God has a great plan for you, and you're doing a great job. I know what! Why don't you start writing everything that's happening? Write a book about your experiences. It's not everyday somebody gets shot in the head, never losing consciousness after being shot three more times, and then lives to tell about it."

"I can't write! Let alone a book!"

"Vonny, before you dismiss the idea, let me tell you what I know. There are so many abused women out there like you going through a rough time. They need to hear how somebody like them made it in the midst of tragedy and sorrow."

"Yeah, but I haven't made it."

"You're alive, aren't you?"

"Yeah, but—"

"There are no 'buts' Vonny. Your book will be a blessing for others and therapy for you. Trust me."

"I'm trying to Rev," I said through sobs.

We talked until I was relaxed and able to laugh. Before hanging up, Reverend Lewis prayed, and I thanked him for his love and faith in me. The next morning after waking my children and taking Sheriah to school, I slowly walked up all those stairs again to my mother's empty apartment to pray, call the Mortgage Company and start writing. I thanked God for the newfound strength—praying to retain the peace I felt. I reached for the phone and called the Mortgage Company. I heard Mr. Ross' voice on the other end and told him who I was.

"Oh, hello Mrs. Grant."

"Good morning, Mr. Ross. Did you find out about my house?"

"Oh, yes. Your policy will be honored. The insurance company will be in touch with you by letter. Just send us the eight hundred and forty dollars towards the August payment and we'll get the rest from your insurance."

"Thank you sweet Jesus!" I screamed after hanging up the phone. "Thank you! Thank you! Thank you!" and hopped up and down on my good foot. Then, I sat down on the couch crying, thanking God again for always making a way for me out of the darkness, in spite of my own faults. I sat there thinking about my life with Herb over the last ten years of our marriage. *What a mess!*

I thought about the three beautiful children God had blessed me with and when Herby and I first got married in August of 1986 and all the dreams and goals we had. We hoped to buy a house—have a new car—have another child—make each other happy—help me finish college and start my own business in whatever. A smile spread across my face because most of that we did, except... I shook my head so that I wouldn't get sad again. I limped to the dining room table to get my pen and pad. I eagerly began writing about all the events of yesterday and every day before that. Rev was right as usual. The writing was doing me a world of good—making possible for me to see my life from a different perspective. I even imagined myself writing a book.

EPILOGUE

NEW BEGINNINGS

Neither my husband nor I knew who we were or where we belonged. We just played a role that we had been taught and tried to work within the boundaries of our existence—bringing all our pains, fears, and wounds to our relationship, and expecting one another to heal them and make everything better. But of course, life doesn't work like that. No one can (not even children) confront your fears, heal your wounds, ease your pains, and bring you joy, happiness, love, and peace, but you and God.

For me, an identity is having a sense of purpose—a sense of belonging—a sense of spirituality—a sense of self, and a sense of God and all that is made available to us: the trees, plants, air, water, animals, people, and life. All these are essential to our everyday development of who we are.

I no longer view my past and present experiences as shameful and embarrassing. I view them as stepping stones to piece together my worth and value of who I am. At times, like now, it's a painful, slow process. Then again, so was not knowing who I was for thirty-four-years. Because of the falsehood of identity I lived with for so long, the very person who I thought gave me my identity almost killed me.

Living through these four years after my husband shot me, I have grown to a fuller understanding of the spiritual process that I was already learning from Reverend Lewis. All that happened to me strengthened me as a person and allowed me to forgive Herby and myself in order to move forward with my children's lives and mine.

If I had not gone through the ten month separation from Herby, lived in a Battered Woman's shelter, struggled on my own in

231

a strange land without any family, friends, or money, I don't believe I would have survived. I can't express enough how happy I am to be alive and how thankful I am to God for His patience, strength, and unconditional love.

The stabbing pain that I carried in my soul after the shooting was so deeply rooted in my heart that it was nearly torn in pieces. Everything about my life seemed like a continuous battle, and I was tired of fighting and needed to feel whole and complete. It would take many sessions of therapy with Rev to help me mend and heal the brokenness of my life. I struggled in those sessions, as I still do today, to maintain my sanity. I also still grieve for all that I lost: my marriage, my husband, and my young girl's image of a perfect family. But, my life was not the only life at stake. Marques, Corey, and Sheriah's lives also needed a level of normalcy and healing. With the power of God, I fought with my demons of depression and guilt over the years to create a new, healthy, and stronger foundation for the sake of my children. They deserved at least that much and more. I could not change our reality, but I could change how we reacted to it.

I had choices—choices that I never knew I had before. I didn't have to accept the roles that society, the church, or others placed on me as a woman and mother just because of my gender. I was free to challenge anything or anyone that limited my potential and boxed me into what they wanted me to be for their own benefit.

The process of learning how to search within my spirit through prayer and meditation while I was separated from my husband enabled me to discover that I had the power within me to love myself in spite of my weaknesses. I learned to overcome any obstacle that I faced; I gathered up the "courage to change the things that I could." In the end, that experience proved to be one of the greatest spiritual tools for the darkest journey that I ever had to travel.

Within these years, God also carved out newer, more exciting, and brighter paths for my children's lives and mine. My oldest child, Marques, has graduated from high school and has begun his second year at one of the most prestigious, all-male, historically black colleges in the nation. Corey and Sheriah appear to be normal, happy eleven and eight-year-olds. (Despite my children's appearances, I am not oblivious to the fact that we still have plenty of healing-work to do, and a tough, but "God-loving" journey ahead of us.) I have become an advocate for other abused women, a board member of the New York State Coalition Against Domestic Violence, and an entrepreneur as a Public Speaker. Oh yeah! I am also a writer! Can you believe that? *I* can't!

I am proud and honored that God has chosen me to do work that is bigger than I could have ever imagined. I continue to affirm myself as a person, woman, and mother through my writing. Writing allowed the healing process to begin in me from within and gave me a place of peace that I can retreat to when I have no control of the pressures outside of myself. Writing has also helped me discover my voice in ways that would never have been possible. Discovering my voice has enabled me to stand for what I believe and the confidence and self-esteem I need to achieve the mission that God has chosen for me on the earth.

With the failings of a governmental, bureaucratic system that has little regard for women and their children, and holds us accountable for our partners' abusive and controlling behaviors, I share my story in the hopes that it will educate, empower other women, especially African-American women and women of color, to know that they are not alone in their everyday struggles for identity, and that it is possible for them to discover their own voices, tell their stories, and claim their freedom, no matter their experiences or ages.

Blessings to all,

Lavon Morris-Grant

Afterword

In some instances I have changed the names of streets and people's names to protect their identities and privacy. Some of the conversations have been re-created, but the story is accurate and conveys my truth from my perspective.

I would love to hear from you with your comments about this book and your own experiences of abuse and recovery.

Lavon Morris-Grant
PMB 219
56 North Plank Road, Suite 1
Newburgh, NY 12550-2116

About the Author

Lavon Morris-Grant is a native of New Jersey, and a graduate of New Jersey City University with a bachelor's degree in Marketing. She is a board member of the New York State Coalition Against Domestic Violence and a nationally known speaker on topics related to abuse. She resides in upstate New York with her three children.

MCS PUBLISHING
www.atlasbooks.com

Quick Order Form

Telephone orders: 1-800-BOOKLOG. Have your credit card ready.
Fax orders: 419-281-6883. Send this form.
email orders: order@bookmaster.com
Postal orders: BookMasters, Inc.
P.O. Box 388
Ashland, OH 44805

Please send me _____ book(s)

Name:_____

Address:_____

City_____State_____Zip_____-_____

Telephone: _____

email address: _____

Sales tax: Please add 6.25% (all New York State residents add 7.25%) and $5.00 shipping & handling

Payment: Check Money Order Credit card:
Visa MasterCard AMEX Discover

Card number:_____

Name on card:_____Exp. date:____/__

MCS PUBLISHING
www.atlasbooks.com

Quick Order Form

Telephone orders: 1-800-BOOKLOG. Have your credit card ready.
Fax orders: 419-281-6883. Send this form.
email orders: order@bookmaster.com
Postal orders: BookMasters, Inc.
　　　　　　　P.O. Box 388
　　　　　　　Ashland, OH 44805

Please send me _____ book(s)

Name:_____

Address:_____

City_____State_____Zip_____-_____

Telephone:　　_____

email address:　　_____

Sales tax:　Please add 6.25% (all New York State residents add 7.25%) and $5.00 shipping & handling

Payment:　Check　Money Order　Credit card:
　　Visa　　MasterCard　　AMEX　　Discover

Card number:_____

Name on card:_____Exp. date:____/__